Pearls of Wisdom

Pearls of Wisdom
For Your Path to Peace

JANE HOLMAN

the kind press

Copyright © 2020 Jane Holman
First published by the kind press, 2020

All rights reserved. No part of this book may be reproduced, stored in a retrieval system or transmitted in any form or by any means, electronic, mechanical photocopying, recording, or otherwise, without written permission from the author and publisher.

This book is written as a source of spiritual guidance only. The advice and information in this book should not be considered a substitute for the advice of a qualified medical professional or registered psychologist. The author and the publisher expressly disclaim responsibility for any adverse effects arising from the use or application of the advice and information in this book.

Cover, internal design and typeset by Elle Lynn.
Author photo by Kristy Lockwood.

Cataloguing-in-Publication entry is available from the National Library Australia.

NATIONAL LIBRARY OF AUSTRALIA

ISBN 978-0-6487927-9-6 (Paperback)
ISBN 978-0-6488706-0-9 (Ebook)

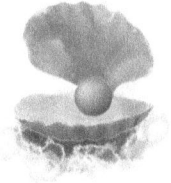

Just as a pearl *transforms* irritation and abrasion into *beauty* and *peace,* so too can *we.*

To Julia and Nic, for your belief in the power
of our combined wisdom and dreams.

To Pete, for your unwavering support,
the unconditional love—and for always
cherishing what I have to say.

Contents

Foreword	*xiii*
Book essence	*xvi*
Introduction	*xii*
Dear Reader—my letter to you	*xxi*
My recommendations for reading this book	*xxiii*

Abundance	1		Chaos	51
Addictions	4		Circle	56
Adventure	7		Comparison	59
Alignment	10		Compassion	62
Amazingness	14		Competition	64
Anxiety	18		Compliments	68
Authenticity	22		Connections	71
Awakening	25		Consuming	73
			Contrasts	76
Beauty	28		Creativity	79
Being a god	32			
Being a goddess	34		Declutter	82
Being uncomfortable	37		Dreams	84
Being unstoppable	40			
Body	43		Ego	87
Books	47		Embarrassing moments	90
Bravery	49		Emotions	93
			Energy	96
			Envy	101

F Family	104	*L* Leaving the planet	170
Fantasy	108	Lessons	173
Fear	110	Life purpose	175
Food	114	Love	177
Forging your path	116		
Forgiveness	120	*M* Magic and miracles	180
Freedom	123	Meaning	184
Friendship	127	Meditation	187
Fun	132	Mindfulness	190
		Mistakes	193
G Go within	137	Mystical experiences	195
Gratitude	140		
		N Nature	202
H Happiness	143		
Healing journey	147	*O* Openness to receiving	205
I Inner child	152	*P* Patience	208
Inspiration	155	Peace	211
Intuition	158	Pedestals	215
		Perfectionism	218
J Joy	161	Possibilities	221
		Power	224
K Keeping confidences	164		
Kindness	167	*Q* Questions	228

Reiki	231	Understanding	293
Resistance	235	Universal guidance	296
Romance	228	Unrequited love	299
Saying goodbye	241	Variety and versatility	301
Self-care	244	Visibility	304
Self-worth	248	Vulnerability	307
Sensuality	253		
Signs and symbols	256	Work	310
Soulmates	260	Worry	313
Spontaneity	263		
Stepping back	266	X-rated or A-rated	316
Stillness	269		
Stress	272	Youthfulness	322
Success	275		
Surrender	278	Zaniness	325
		Zzz … sleep	327
Thoughts	280		
Transformation	283		
Travel	287		
Trusting your future	290		

Afterword — *331*
Acknowledgements — *332*
About the Author — *336*

Foreword

Jane and I met years ago, via email, and although I don't remember when she first emailed me, I do know that every time I saw her name pop up in my inbox over the years, I would smile.

A beloved teacher and mentor in my life once helped me see that the best kind of mentor/mentee relationship is one that is reciprocal. Without ever placing one or the other on a pedestal, you maintain a sense of equilibrium that supports the intention of growth and expansion, while inviting a fluid and evolving energy that allows both of you to teach the other, in some form.

Suffice to say, while Jane and I have worked together over the years—through my various courses, programs, books and other offerings—when I opened her beautiful book for the first time, I knew she would be teaching, guiding and coaching me through something wonderful, important and deeply healing.

Tears streamed down my face during my first reading of her book. In one specific chapter, early on in the book, she spoke so clearly, directly and lovingly to something that had been bothering me for weeks, and with her loving words, I could finally let go of something that needed to be released. I knew then, that the rest of the book held so much magic for me too.

I was hungry for more of Jane's soothing words, and as I worked my way slowly through chapter after chapter, I remember a sense of peace and calm starting to wash over me; after a busy week, I truly felt like I was dropping into my body again. It became clear my body, mind and soul were so receptive to her work and her words, and I was embodying everything she was writing about and guiding me to uncover, believe and receive.

Jane writes from the heart and soul, but also from something deeper and higher; she receives wisdom and guidance that teaches us how to see our own greatness, as well as how to access it, even (and especially) through adversity or challenging times. She doesn't ask you to try to look, feel or be perfect, but rather, to acknowledge that sometimes what might seem hurtful can actually help you heal.

We worked together on her book proposal, and after so many years of emailing, I don't know who was more excited that we were finally meeting one another, albeit online.

While on our call, Jane was bathed in the most brilliant indigo and purple light. I was mesmerised throughout the 3-hour workshop and I actually took screenshots to send to her. I kept telling her she had this beautiful purple light all around her, and even her hair and clothes looked purple. She told me she was actually wearing a black top, and there was no purple in her room. But—just like the indigo of the third eye chakra and how it relates to intuition and clarity—I believe the purple that was coming through the screen was a clear and powerful sign of the clarity, purpose and intuitive support this book will bring to each and every reader who reads Jane's words.

In our email correspondence afterwards, she wrote to tell me this book was to be published, in a deal she had inked just 10 days after our workshop. She said, 'Who would have ever thought things could happen with such ease and pace! Every step seems to just take care of itself every day.' I remember thinking: *That's what happens when you're in alignment, and Jane, you're the embodiment of this.* I replied and told her the absolute truth: 'You're so ready for this.'

Beautiful Jane, I'm so beyond grateful you have written this book for all of us to read, learn from, and cherish. Thank you for trusting the timing of your work, and for being brave enough to share it with us. And thank you too, for emailing me all those years ago. It is such an honour and privilege to know you.

Beautiful reader, now it's your turn to discover the pearls of wisdom in this book, by (re)discovering the pearls of wisdom within yourself. So, get settled, dive in, and find your own path to peace.

- *Cassie Mendoza-Jones*
Author of *Aligned and Unstoppable*,
You Are Enough and *It's All Good*
Kinesiologist, Coach and Speaker

Book essence

Life to me is purely a reflection of what we are willing to see, be, receive, think and learn. Life continually calls us to look within to connect with our own wisdom. We can't know peace until we know ourselves well enough to get free of all that limits us—under all our stuff is our bliss. All the wisdom we require to successfully navigate life is within. The challenge is to develop a clear pathway for accessing all that we are and all that we know. Access to our wisdom is peace—peace within and peace in life. Understanding how we respond to life gives us the opportunity to change and let go of what does not serve us.

This book is about turning all that life presents us with into our wisdom and ensuing peace. This includes the suffering, the difficulties, the joy and the miracles—and our reactions to it all. Our reactions and responses to life are our teachers. Our wisdom—the knowledge of how we can respond to life optimally—can form the foundation for an enduring peace that flows into all areas of our lives.

The pearls of wisdom in this book contain much of what I have lived and reacted to in life and subsequently turned into opportunities for insight. Each time I access new wisdom my self-worth, self-knowledge, power and inner peace flourish.

Introduction

Spirituality, and finding our inner light, wisdom and peace, is an evolution in consciousness for everyone: it is on our own terms in our own way. The answers are all within. However, accessing our inner wisdom is not a linear process. Moments of awakening and insight occur in unique and often unexpected ways. *Pearls of Wisdom: For Your Path to Peace* provides sparks of potential insight to open doors to consciousness for us at all stages of the journey within. Peace comes when our inner wisdom is heard rather than the constant demands of the ego.

We have all at times been wounded and irritated by life. Over time, after much abrasion, beautiful pearls are created within oysters. We too can transform irritation into wisdom and then peace. Through adversity, we have an opportunity to transmute our suffering into wisdom, if we are willing to acknowledge the lessons inherent in the trials and tribulations of life. On the other side of our limitations (often self-imposed) are our wisdom, peace and true potential.

This book is about transforming our challenges and irritations into our own pearls of wisdom. Wisdom is beauty; we glow with it. Having access to all our learned wisdom brings inner peace and worth. Peace and wisdom combine to give us freedom from fear and the demands of the ego; from here we get to live from our hearts. In these times (and beyond) more than ever we need to access our own inner well of wisdom and peace. Our wisdom and peace keep us in alignment with our highest good and our higher selves. Wisdom is acquired after knowledge, insight and experience combine repeatedly throughout our lives. Our wisdom evolves after learning and healing, often through challenge and adversity. Wisdom is power as we know our true selves and can access our greatness. With wisdom come self-awareness, self-worth and the ultimate: peace, as we know ourselves, and we are comfortable with that. There is great peace in knowing one's wisdom is available at all times, in all situations. Living in a state of peace affects all those we connect with. One peaceful person can create peace in another. We need the world to be filled with peaceful people who change others, one person at a time, with their calming presence. When we strive for inner peace and use the tips (for moving forward on the path to peace) within this book, we move closer to peace being our natural state.

Wisdom is the precursor for peace to reign in our lives. Inner wisdom is the fuel that generates peace. There is a contentment that comes with acknowledging the wisdom that we have acquired throughout all the highs, lows and upheaval experienced in life. Inner wisdom generates light and the peace we radiate can be witnessed and felt by others. There is a wisdom and peace in knowing where you've been, who you are and where you're headed. As self-worth grows, peace is more easily attained as we become wise enough to choose thinking and words that promote peace. With wisdom we know that there is a choice in any moment to look through the eyes of love or fear. From the space of wisdom and peace we become masters of our own destiny as we consistently co-create with divine connection. Wisdom is empowerment.

Many people cite happiness as a desired state. Peace is the cornerstone of happiness. Without inner peace, happiness is determined by the external world and is often short-lived. Peace is the essential starting point to build the foundation and momentum for happiness to flourish. Peace doesn't mean living without experiences of turmoil—it means that within us, there is still a place of calm in which to deal with what life presents. Peace that has arisen through our wisdom is enduring. It is a background contentment that is always there once we have cleared the way for its presence.

I have lived (and continue to live) the messages and wisdom that I am imparting within these pages. My wisdom and yours continue to evolve daily. This is my wisdom, from my healing journey so far. For me wisdom and peace have come from all that I've experienced in life, including all the chaos and suffering. I have been in the tough places; I've felt and experienced what life can throw at us. There is always light on the other side through our own wisdom. Suffering turns into wisdom after we have grasped the learning and insight provided by some of our most challenging experiences. I have been forced to seek wisdom and peace in order to thrive rather than just survive on our planet of contrasts. Many friends, family members, colleagues and clients have repeatedly asked me throughout life, 'What is your secret? You radiate peace and worth. You're content, optimistic. You always seem so aware—you know what's going on within you and others.' This book is in response to such comments throughout my life. These pages share the insights and healing that I have had to activate and acknowledge within me in order to create what I've always desired in life: wisdom, peace, joy and fulfilment. I have acquired the wisdom to know that so much more is possible, and the inner peace to continue trusting in the process of learning through life.

Moments of wisdom and peace can occur in all situations and at any time. *Pearls of Wisdom: For Your Path to Peace* provides many themes and scenarios that you may identify with or relate to and can then embrace as opportunities to deepen levels of both wisdom and peace within you. There are many threads of commonality throughout the pearls of wisdom and repetition of key messages. This is designed to encourage life-enhancing ways of being to be fully integrated into the psyche.

Dear Reader – my letter to you

Dear Reader,

Congratulations on allowing your inner guidance to bring you to the treasures within these pages. You are a brave soul who is ready to turn whatever life has presented to you into greater wisdom and beautiful, ensuing peace. May these pearls of wisdom unlock even more of your potential, power and peace. You are ready and it is time—your time. I have lived or experienced all that is within these pages. As we are all in this together, I imagine life has also presented you with many relatable scenarios. My path to peace, my evolving healing and transformation through wisdom, is yours.

I welcome you to the new wisdom and peace that will flow into your life upon immersing yourself in the messages within these pages.

I hope that each pearl of wisdom opens you to new ways of thinking and of perceiving yourself and your world. I hope ripples of change and inspiration are stirred within you.

I know that your self-worth will be enhanced as you experience 'I've got this' moments.

May you feel empowered and proud of the inner wisdom you are accessing.

I pray that the wisdom that comes with your inner work rewards you with both inner peace and peace in your life.

May your challenges and healing evolve into wisdom.

May your new-found peace further power your potential and wisdom.

Jane Holman

My recommendations for reading this book

Pearls of Wisdom: For Your Path to Peace can be read from cover to cover at a pace that allows you to integrate each pearl of wisdom. Or you may like to select one that you know you do well and attempt to do even better; there is always room for improvement—we are constant works in progress. Alternatively, you may like to select a pearl that you know requires some commitment and keep that in the forefront of your mind for several days to practise and integrate. You may choose to highlight areas that particularly resonate for you - for later reflection. You may choose a pearl a day to focus on for the day just because it calls to you.

Embrace the affirmations and the tips for moving forward on the path to peace to further deepen your understanding and the integration of key teachings. Each essence provides an abridged version of each pearl to help clarify key insights. You may like to choose some of these from time to time to keep as reminders in your phone notes, or in your journal.

This book can also be used as an oracle if you ask questions before opening the book at the page you've been guided too. Flick open the book and trust you will land on the pearl that is just right for you, for your highest good, in this moment, to keep moving forward.

Some questions before using the book as an oracle may be:
>What do I need to know for my highest good today?
>What pearl do I need to integrate into my life to keep moving forward?
>What would bring more fun to my life?
>What would help me connect with others more joyfully?
>What would help me access my life purpose more quickly?
>What do I need to know to more fully access my talents and abilities?
>What lesson do I need to grow in peace this day?
>What could I change today that would set me free?
>What piece of wisdom can open doors of change for me this day?

You will notice some common themes throughout the snippets. This is intentional, as important concepts require consolidation over time and need to be presented in new contexts to become understood and inherent.

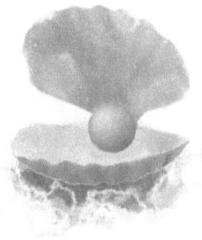

Abundance

BELIEVE AND FEEL AS THOUGH IT ALREADY EXISTS.

Abundance is more than just money. It is a plethora of what lights us up. Be proud of your abundance. Abundance is love in our lives, inner peace, great connections, fulfilling work and relationships, adventure, surprises, and time to spend on things that inspire us.

Abundance is closely tied to our perception of freedom: being able to do, be, have, create and go wherever and whenever we choose. When immersed in and connected with abundance, we trust that the universe is behind us, always supporting us and providing us with what we require for our highest good. We need to consistently work on the inner belief that we are deserving. If we don't truly believe we are worthy of receiving, it is more difficult to manifest what we desire.

Abundance leads to peace as we have a level of comfort and satisfaction in our lives that pleases us. More than likely we have satisfying and inspiring work that we get well paid for. Make sure you accept and expect the right financial reward for your work.

Being financially abundant allows us to be generous and make a difference in the lives of others. Making your passion your profession promotes abundance.

If we are willing to make self-care and self-worth a priority, we feel great and naturally attract abundance and positive cash flows into our lives. Abundance and joy are high vibration states. Maintaining a feeling of joy and wealth (even if it hasn't quite arrived) helps draw it in at a more rapid rate. Use your imagination to perceive that state or situation you dream about (as if it's already happened or is here) to help bring forth the abundance you are seeking. What I have found is that if I hold a desire strongly enough and connect it with positive, excited and joyful emotions, the desire finds its way to me in some way, shape or form. As Esther and Abraham Hicks say, 'the universe expands to match desires'. I have most fortunately found this to be true.

Having gratitude for all that you are, all that you have, everything you've experienced and everywhere you've been is a sure-fire way to build the energy of abundance in your life. Trust that what is meant for you will come. Be willing to let go of what is not destined for you and release what doesn't serve you (for your highest good). This makes the space for the abundance that is yours to reveal itself.

Affirmation

I am truly grateful for all that I am and all that I have. The universe wishes to give to me all that my heart desires for my highest good. I am ready to receive.

My tip for your path to peace

Even if you haven't yet created the level of abundance that you require and desire, maintain the feeling of joy and gratitude that you associate with abundance to bring it forth more rapidly. Freedom from excessive striving creates peace.

The essence

Abundance brings peace as we enjoy a level of comfort and success that pleases us. We trust that we are always provided for. Our self-worth is enhanced accordingly, which further brings forth and attracts more peace.

Live with constant thoughts and feelings of abundance and eventually the universe will catch up and provide abundance aplenty.

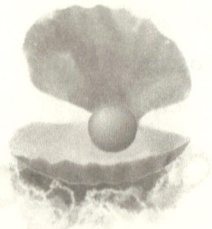

Addictions

JOY IS A NATURAL PRECURSOR TO PEACE AND AN ANTIDOTE FOR ADDICTION.

Addiction is avoiding where we are currently at by using (often unhealthy) numbing experiences. These can also numb our potential in life. Addiction can happen when our personal cup isn't full of self-worth, inspiration and purpose. For some the void is filled with alcohol, drugs or cigarettes (anything to dull the feeling that something is not quite right within us or our lives). For some it may be shopping. Spending excessive and unaffordable amounts of money on clothes and creating beautiful looks could also be unexpressed creativity attempting to unleash itself. The key is to look 'within' the addiction to ascertain what is really going on with us. If we are free of addictive tendencies, we may be able to perceive the creativity that is truly calling.

Become aware of any motivations behind addictive tendencies: shining light on these areas helps us to gain freedom from habitual and limiting patterns. As soon as we identify any form of addiction, we have a chance of getting free of it and moving to a new space. Each 'failed attempt' at breaking free of addiction is a win in disguise. Each unsuccessful attempt moves us one step closer to freedom. With each intention to quit we are putting our mind, body and spirit on notice that we plan to overcome any barrier to success … and we will. It takes practice, patience, willingness and celebration of each attempt, regardless of results. Non-judgement is key. Self-worth is often low when we are in the grip of an addiction, so we need to work hard at supporting and nurturing ourselves.

We also need to find what is truly under the addiction. What is it giving us temporary reprieve from looking at, or taking responsibility for, or fighting to get free of? There is something that we have disowned, and this aspect is unique to all of us. The only way out of it is to move through it with awareness, honesty and kindness to self. This is a time to be vulnerable (which is strength in disguise) and seek support. There are many avenues of support today; it is a matter of seeking what works for each individual. Reiki and other forms of energy healing are great assistants to overcoming addiction, as they can bypass the mind and heal from the inside out.

Follow what lights you up and find joy in something that isn't costing you your health, relationships and finances. Inspiration and motivation are great distractions from addiction.

Affirmation

I am stronger than I ever allowed myself to believe. I easily get free of anything I set my intention on.

> **My tip for your path to peace**
>
> Look within to discover what the addiction is hiding and at the same time (with equal intent) look for what brings you joy. Joy is a great healer of addictions. Without addiction greater peace can prevail.

The essence

Create a full personal cup by taking care of your inner world, health and wellbeing. From here there will then be less chance of craving things from the outside world to fill you up.

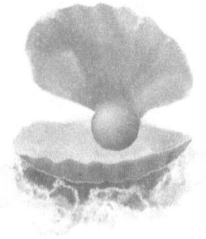

Adventure

NOURISHMENT FOR SPIRIT.

Adventure can be defined as an unusual, exciting or daring experience. Adventure is about letting life unfold on life's terms—embracing the unknown and expecting the unexpected. Adventure is an antidote for a mundane, frustrating existence and contributes to a peaceful, content or creative way of being. The great thing about adventure is that it can happen anytime, anywhere. All you need to do is stay open to opportunities for fun, love and personal growth. Personal growth is the adventure of a lifetime, unlocking the aspects of ourselves that enable us to develop greater wisdom, peace and elevated emotions, enhancing our lives.

What is inspiration and adventure for you? Could it be going within to discover what it is that is truly amazing about you, or holding you back? Is it a trip to that exotic foreign country you've always dreamed about? Is it learning to dance, fly, cook or write?

If we do the same thing over again, we often get the same results. Adventure means we are doing or experiencing something differently, bringing new life along with it. Embracing adventure means that we are likely to experience the joy that creates positive energy for receiving new opportunities. The new thinking associated with adventure also changes us and our lives; such is the power of our thoughts. Allow space, by releasing the old to make way for the new, for the magical unknown to enter. Holding on too tightly to the old makes it difficult to welcome the new. Old ways don't encourage us to open new doors. Be willing to close all those doors that are leading you nowhere and no longer light you up: it's time for new adventures.

There is an abundance of things to inspire us on this gorgeous planet. Why not take advantage of the infinite potential for adventure - and be open to new possibilities? Any form of adventure excites the soul and creates the space for possibilities to flow in. Be brave and take a chance on a new adventure. You and your life will thank you for it.

Affirmation

I freely add new experiences and adventure in unimaginable forms to my daily living.

My tip for your path to peace

A peaceful life is created when we go in directions that feel light and right. Adventure has an element of stepping into the unknown and contributes to peace as we are present and have surrendered control, in favour of expecting the unexpected.

The essence

Frustration and irritation occur when we do the same things repeatedly, without experiencing any joy or contentment. Adventure allows us to go in new directions and experience new inspiration. It helps to unlock more of our untapped potential. Embracing adventure and change leads to more change and a bigger life.

Alignment

OUR BREATHTAKING SPACE OF CONNECTION.

Alignment for me is remembering that I am a spiritual being having a human experience and at the same time connecting with my divine source. It is the space where we connect to the infinite possibilities and magnificent abundance of the universe. It is where magic, miracles and love originate.

When in alignment I am peaceful and content. I don't sweat the small stuff, and my faith in the divine plan and my ability to co-create with the universe is high. I feel deeply connected to my life purpose. I have a greater sense of who I am and where I am going. My self-worth is higher because I perceive my own light and can appreciate the difference I am making for others. The more time I spend in alignment the easier it is to perceive when I'm out of alignment. From here I take steps (usually just a change in thinking and more gratitude) to move back into alignment.

In alignment, nature makes me feel alive. I feel beautifully connected to all the plants, birds and animals around me. In the space of nature, I connect with the expansiveness of me, rather than the smallness. The peace and creativity in nature uplift and inspire me. In fact, after fifteen minutes in my garden, I was able to capture in this pearl what alignment means for me. Thank you nature!

I am more creative and inspired when in alignment. My ideas flow, I flow and life flows. Problems have an incredible way of dissolving into solutions. My intuition becomes my ever-faithful guide as I can connect to this guidance with greater ease.

The most peaceful aspect of being in alignment is that my emotions are in check. I feel that I am being the best version of myself. I'm not reacting or being governed by the voice and demands of the ego. My health and wellbeing are heightened. I am extremely present, and at the same time perceive a greater future with unlimited possibilities.

When alignment becomes our dominant way of being, if we do react, worry or give into stress, we can more readily come back to our aligned state. Practice, commitment and intent are all important here.

When out of alignment (which happens regularly and repeatedly) we need to determine what works for us to restore it … and our sanity. I find simply catching it, and acknowledging it, immediately helps. As soon as I react to something or someone and feel my connection slipping, I stop, breathe, assess what emotions I'm experiencing, acknowledge them (and what is underneath them) without judging, and as soon as possible reach for better-feeling thoughts and emotions. I seek distraction in a positive way. Writing, journaling, focusing on what I'm grateful for, exercise or being in nature are great forms of 'distraction' for me. I ask to surrender the situation and say things like 'I let go and let my team take over', 'I ask to reconnect with my divine source immediately', or 'I stand still and connect with my power within', or 'I step back and let loving guidance show me the way'. Whatever feels light and right for you is your best way back to your alignment with source.

Work continually on feeling good, peaceful and happy. Follow what lights you up to feel good. Make fun a priority. Whenever you are feeling good you are in alignment. When in alignment we draw to ourselves what the heavens wish us to receive for our highest good, healing and growth. We get to shine brighter and encourage others to do the same.

Affirmation

*I trust the barometer that exists
within me to show me when
I move out of alignment.
Moving back into alignment
is my new default system.
It occurs with ease, grace and love.*

> **My tip for your path to peace**
>
> Alignment is peace. Make the commitment to always come back to alignment as soon as possible in the way that is most effective and enduring for you. Build your levels of peace and joy as often as you can, as they provide the foundation for quickly moving back into alignment.

The essence

Alignment is our divine birthright. It is our true way of functioning as an infinite, expansive, spiritual being having an earthly experience.

Amazingness

REFUSE TO ALLOW MOMENTS OF
REACTION TO DIM YOUR LIGHT AND
LOWER YOUR BEAUTIFUL VIBRATION.
SHINE BRIGHT.

Discovering our amazingness is a lifetime body of work. It could be likened to going on an archaeological dig to find all our lost treasures and those parts of ourselves that we may have disowned. Both do us a disservice. Being unable to acknowledge our worth and refusing to look at our shadow aspects equally limit us and our potential. Each time we journey within and learn more about ourselves we grow in self-worth, wisdom and peace.

Embracing our amazingness is also about acknowledging the magnificence of the journey so far. Each mistake we have 'allowed' ourselves to make has given us the opportunity to learn something new and to pivot in a new direction consistent with how we perceive ourselves. Each time we confront an aspect of our behaviour, attitudes and thought patterns that are harmful to ourselves and others, we get greater freedom, and take one step closer to becoming the amazing beings we truly are.

People (and more importantly our reactions to them) are our greatest gifts and teachers when wishing to access our true potential.

Every judgement and negative reaction is a chance to dive within to discover what this person is triggering and bringing to the surface for us to look at. Behind every reaction there is always information and potential freedom from our limitations.

Bursts of amazingness often come after moments of severe discomfort with how we are behaving or thinking. A revelation arose for me when I realised I was negatively triggered when people duplicated my ideas (or shoes). My reaction was always along the lines of 'Why can't they be more original?' With this ego-dominated response, I was inadvertently engaging in competition, judgement and feelings of inadequacy, as part of my self-worth was obviously connected to being separate, different or original in some way. In all of this I was limiting my personal growth. Now, when people duplicate anything connected with me, I look through eyes of love and peace and see them as the innocents they truly are. In their own way they are seeking to be more and have more. Maybe they haven't yet found their own inner guidance system, self-worth and personal power. I took my time to find my way, so I can respect the process others need to go through. We often duplicate those we admire until we find our own voice and our own way. This is more than okay. We are all in this together. Some day we may be the inspiration for an individual we once admired.

Getting free of this 'imitation reaction' has allowed me to access more of my amazingness and be willing to step up and lead. Now when I hear the saying 'Imitation is the greatest form of flattery', rather than it pushing my buttons, I'm willing to own that someone has looked to me for inspiration and guidance. I now feel honoured rather than irritated.

Resist any inclination to make yourself 'smaller or less than' in an attempt to make other people feel more secure around you. The world needs us to be expansive and bright to most effectively serve the world.

Be kind to yourself when attempting to see and perceive your amazingness. This can be a struggle as we can become so accustomed to how we function and who we are—that if we are told we are amazing, it may not initially register. The beautiful soul who has spoken their truth about our amazingness may be met with blank stares. Be gracious and receive the compliment and then work to see yourself through the eyes of another. If I was told I was amazing or incredible, I would often have to ask my husband why? It's great to have someone we trust remind us every now and then—particularly one that adores us. Don't worry if you can't see greatness in yourself for a while (even a long while) as it takes work and a continual effort to change our perceptions. We have to change our conditioned thinking by filling our minds with fresh thinking about ourselves. If you aren't quite there yet, it doesn't mean you don't have great self-worth; it's just that there's so much more of you to discover and appreciate. There is nothing wrong with you. You are complex. You are perfection unfolding.

Affirmation

*I trust my inner guide
to shine light on my limitations
and greatness, so I may access
my true potential.*

My tip for your path to peace

Make truth at the centre of all self-reflection. Ask 'What am I unwilling or unable to see right now?' Giving up resistance to what is revealed brings forth peace.

The essence

Discovering and embracing our amazingness is the healing journey of a lifetime. Enjoy the unfolding. It is designed perfectly for you.

Anxiety

FIND THE WISDOM AND GIFTS UNDERNEATH IT.

Anxiety … is it friend or foe? Much of our response to anxiety can come down to how we view it. We need to befriend our anxiety and not judge ourselves for the experience of it. There is often wisdom underneath it. We can't let it define us or limit us in any way. We need to release all resistance to being free of anxiety and to feeling good, knowing in our hearts that we are worthy of peace and contentment.

Anxiety happens in varying extremes, often to highly sensitive, creative and intuitive people. It can be part of our inner guidance system, our intuition letting us know that something doesn't feel quite right. It can be a way to generate change and to get things done, as anything that we are avoiding can trigger feelings of anxiety. Resistance and procrastination are not friends of anxiety. Surrender, on the other hand, is.

Anxiety has many triggers often unique to every individual. Getting to know your anxiety and working with it is essential.

Professional help is often required to determine whether there are underlying health issues causing it. For me, gluten, caffeine and alcohol are triggers. A lovely glass of wine or two feels great initially and then as the relaxing feelings wear off a background sense of anxiety kicks in. This alcohol-fuelled anxiety usually involves me in replaying the whole night (with me in the most unfavourable light) and simultaneously judging myself for everything I did or said, often with no grounds for any of it. There would be a feeling of wrongness that I would attempt to find reasons for—it felt hideous. Somehow alcohol gives free rein to the mean ego voice in my head, the one that I usually liked to keep dormant. I find an occasional wine is okay—it's better at lunchtime and after I've eaten. My body seems to process it with more ease, which is great as I so enjoy a celebratory sparkling and a catch-up wine with a friend. I do, however, prefer to be a cup-of-tea girl! She's much nicer to me! Caffeine makes me feel so on edge and wound up that I cannot sleep for twenty-four hours. My heart races and my inner calm has been stolen. My advice is to listen to your body. It knows how you can have what you like, in balanced ways that work for you both.

For many sensitive people, avoiding certain situations or people may initially help. It's important to desensitise (at a gradual rate) so that we do not have to isolate ourselves. Reactions to anxiety only increase its intensity and hold. We need a toolkit of tips and tricks to use when anxious feelings descend. I find meditation, deep breathing, connecting with nature, reiki, essential oils, positive affirmations, herbal teas (like chamomile and lemon balm) and acupuncture to be effective.

Energy-sensitive people need to spend time in nature, walking barefoot on the earth, taking salt baths or swimming in the ocean. These simple things clear stored energies that may have been taken on from others. If you are not feeling peace within, there's a fair chance you may have taken something on for someone else. We often unwittingly take on emotions for others, often not knowing the difference between our experience and that of another person. When feelings of anxiety arise always ask to 'return to sender with light and love' anything you've taken on from others.

Affirmation

*I easily perceive the message
my anxiety is giving me,
and then freely release
anxious feelings from
my mind and body.*

My tip for your path to peace

Protect your energies by blessing any space you enter. Affirm that your energetic boundaries are protected and surround yourself with divine white light. Learn to say no and be very aware of where and with whom you are spending your time. Breathe in peace and divine light and breathe out everything that is not, imagining the negative energies leaving your body.

The essence

Work with your anxiety and identify your triggers. Access the wisdom, emotion or message underneath the anxiety for personal growth and as a way forward on your healing journey.

Authenticity

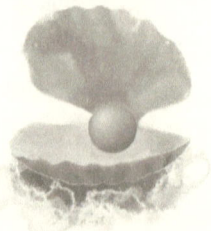

TRUE PEACE IS FOUND IN DISCOVERING WHO YOU ARE AND BEING THAT.

Authenticity means freedom. Freedom to be ourselves. That is all facets of ourselves, not just those we have decided are socially acceptable. We give ourselves permission to stand out (if we so choose) and to fully embrace what brings us joy, regardless of the reactions of others. We can't access our own unique form of greatness if we are attempting to replicate someone else (or the masses), and the world needs our greatness.

> 'You can't be authentic unless you are following your bliss.'
> Dr Wayne Dyer

For me, being authentic was (and still is) the way to access my power, as I am not holding back the aspects of me that I'd decided might be 'too much' for people. When we refuse to be the authentic version of ourselves, we will often go to the wrongness of us, divorcing our true natures to be more like someone else, to fit in. Being ourselves leads to new life. Some people in your life may go away as they relate (more) to the less authentic you;

however, fun new connections often arise as people are drawn to the authentic you.

Being authentic has allowed me to respond to my intuition and to do and be what I needed to be. From here I could learn, grow and access happiness and peace. I have been able to connect more authentically with others. Give up contracting and staying small to fit in (and saying or being what you think others need from you) but instead expand and shine your light. You will give others the inspiration to also be authentic.

Being authentic indicates that you've done the work on your self-worth to the point where all of you is enough, and that is exactly what those around you and the world need. It is a joyful space to occupy, as there's nothing to hide, disown or fear. When you choose to be authentic, you energetically give others the permission to be themselves too. We then have more people stepping into their power and shining their light. It creates a ripple effect that is beautifully contagious. Being willing to be your true self means that you have achieved a level of self-worth that you can be truly proud of. This means you will more likely attract the right situations and people to your 'tribe' to further bring you alive.

Being your authentic self and not requiring validation from anyone is both powerful and peaceful. Being authentic allows us to embrace our differences and uniqueness and to be at peace with that. Our authenticity can be intimidating for some and refreshing for others. Don't dim your light for anyone as you have too much to offer for that. Be okay if another withdraws from your life because they can't handle the real you. That's okay because you get to live your life and follow what lights you up. Others may be inspired by you and step into being more of who they can be. There is greatness in forging your own path and moving away from the flock. Being different and authentic means choosing what works for you, even if it doesn't look like anything anyone else is doing or being. Develop your courage to step up and be different.

Affirmation

I choose to be the light, bright, expansive and authentic me in all situations and with all people.

My tip for your path to peace

Devote time to discovering everything that is great about you, and be that. There is great peace in being comfortable in your own skin and not needing to imitate others.

The essence

You are free and peaceful when you get to be everything that is amazing about you, without self-judgement. You and everyone around you will shine brighter through authenticity.

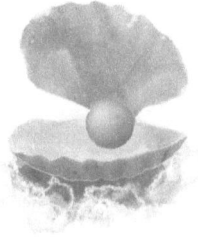

Awakening

TO BE TRULY AWAKE IS
TO TRULY SEE.

Every moment of every day presents a myriad of opportunities to open and step boldly through new doors of perception and healing on the physical, spiritual, emotional and mental levels. Ask yourself regularly, 'What can I see and perceive today, that I've been unwilling or unable to see and perceive?' Make a commitment to see through fresh, new eyes and stay open to new points of view and greater self-knowledge.

Moments of awakening occur when we suspend all forms of judgement and preconditioned responses and be extremely present with what is. We require quieting moments to access this space. Meditation is a direct way to access this quiet place of inner knowing and untapped potential. We move beyond our human perception and tap into the ancient wisdom within us. We access our higher selves and universal intelligence. It is from here that we truly feel the presence of something beyond our earthly existence. We can access insights, wisdom and inspiration when we connect within and to our higher selves. Talents, abilities and possibilities that may have been previously dormant can emerge. We can co-create our lives with divine assistance. We experience unparalleled trust in the universe. Peace prevails as we inherently know that every experience is designed to move us forward on our path of awakening.

For many of us, including myself, the greatest moments of revelation and awakening have occurred after suffering. Sometimes we need to be a little 'cracked open' for the light to flow in. Many of us experience our own greatness after coming through tumultuous times. We are not given anything in life that we can't handle—time, hindsight, kindness to self, forgiveness and reflection on our choices and experiences help us to understand this. Be open to what life presents to fully access the learning and message that has been expertly crafted just for you.

Affirmation

Every moment I am open to awakening to the full realm of understanding of both my earthly and spiritual lives.

My tip for your path to peace

Suspend control and the need to be right whenever you can. This will allow divine wisdom to find the cracks needed to flow through you. Being committed to being right clouds our vision and inner wisdom. Awakening means peace as you gain clarity on who you are and what you require to heal.

The essence

Awakening occurs throughout our lifetimes on an hourly, weekly, monthly or yearly basis as we are open to it. To be open is to be free of set points of view and judgements that prevent us from seeing through illusions to the truth. We need to exist as a question, not always needing answers, or to be right.

What else can I truly see and perceive this day that I have been unwilling or unable to perceive and see?

Beauty

ALLOW YOURSELF TO TRULY SEE …

Beauty is everywhere if we are open to experiencing it. We always have the choice to connect with and be 'beauty'. Beauty provides one of life's contrasts: outer beauty versus inner beauty. Which one is more captivating and enduring? The outer costume can be initially compelling and intoxicating. However, have you noticed how some people become even more beautiful or handsome as you really get to know them? That's because their inner light is strong and you are responding with gratitude to their inner world, their presence. There are many types of physical beauty, including the flowering, youthful beauty and the ageless beauty that comes with the willingness to see beauty everywhere in life and in others.

Take some time in all your connections to truly 'see' beauty and give yourself the same level of vision and kindness. Ask to see the beauty and light in yourself and others. Ask also that they see the beauty and light within you. Inner peace, confidence, light and humour are enduring forms of beauty. Avoid deciding that if someone in your presence has beauty, then you can't. Remove this attempt to dim yourself from your repertoire, by remembering that in a garden all the flowers have permission to bloom: the roses don't decide to wilt just because the sunflowers are radiating—there is room for all to show their unique beauty.

I think physically beautiful people serve a far greater purpose than we realise, challenging us to embrace rather than reject beauty. Rejection of beauty is evident when we decide we are not, or never could be, beautiful in comparison to another. Beautiful people (on the inside and out) can light us up if we allow it, as they can challenge us to rise up and connect with beauty and to see and claim our own beauty. We need to acknowledge that there are infinite forms of beauty. We need not shrink or judge ourselves as less than in the face of beauty.

The most over-the-top and seemingly unreachable versions of beauty that I have encountered have been in the glossy (airbrushed) magazines. One day as I was admiring these almost other-worldly versions of beauty, I was guided to say to myself, 'She is me, I am she, we are one'. The gift of this little mantra was that it immediately created inner peace and dissolved any barriers I had placed between me and the beauty of another, not just in magazines but in life in general. This mantra gave me freedom from separation. If we have allowed someone's beauty to intimidate us, it is important not to allow it to then give us permission to separate from them, or to cut them down in any way. This type of response often comes into play as an attempt to make us feel free of unfavourable and uncomfortable comparison with beautiful individuals. Somehow, it's supposed to make us feel good enough to be present in the company of beauty, but it always makes us feel awful afterwards, as we've moved away from love and into lower vibrational responses. It's crazy stuff, but if we draw attention to some of the limiting unconscious programs we have running us, we can get free. Often, it is an individual's light and presence that we are responding to, and our reactions are in fact a reminder to shine our own light even brighter.

Focus on the beauty around you. Connecting with the beauty in our surroundings helps us to connect with our own beauty and the beauty of others. So much of our lives are consumed by 'busyness'. If we could just stop and take a moment (or many) to truly look around and see the beauty around us, life would take on new meaning and joy. Take a walk in a garden and see the beauty and complexity in nature. Truly see the smiles on the faces of loved ones. Fill your home and office with beautiful things as a constant reminder to keep looking for and focusing on beauty.

An appreciation of beauty in all its forms encourages us to be in a state of gratitude. Joy follows gratitude. Joy will be far less elusive if we make gratitude a daily practice. Find your definitions and expressions of beauty and nurture and embrace them whenever you can. Being able to see and appreciate beauty allows you to connect with it in all moments and places.

Affirmation

I allow myself to see the beauty within me and open to truly seeing the beauty that surrounds me.

> **My tip for your path to peace**
>
> Take time to truly see the light within yourself and others. Be free of definitions of beauty that don't uplift you or give you a sense of peace.

The essence

Beauty radiating from within (our inner light) is more captivating and enduring than our exterior costumes, no matter how lovely they may be. Connect with and embrace all the beauty around you to activate it even more deeply within yourself.

Being a god

BE THE BEST VERSION OF YOU AND
YOU'RE ALREADY THERE.

To be a 'god' and a match for any true 'goddess', one needs to practise what one deems to be godlike behaviours. This could include: valuing integrity; being kind to self and others; respecting women; expressing your truth in a way that is received by others; valuing assertion rather than aggression; expressing emotions; identifying needs for personal growth and striving towards them; finding humour whenever possible; listening rather than just speaking; showing you care; expressing love; and knowing that being vulnerable and seeking support is a sign of strength.

Consistently stepping into being the man you know you can be is a sure-fire way to access your godlike potential. Modelling by positive example for your fellow men (the ways you treat the women in your life) will create more 'gods'. It will also encourage all the potential goddesses around you to step into being all they desire to be and all they can be. This is the power of a supportive and loving man.

It has been said that the quality of a culture or country is indicated by how women are treated, valued and respected. This starts within the family and also within the work family. Over many years of teaching, I often asked fathers of amazing, young respectful boys what their secrets were. The general theme was zero tolerance of disrespect or aggression towards any female members of the family. These young men were already prepared on many levels to lead by example and to become future 'gods' with fulfilling futures. They had every chance of accessing their full potential and creating wonderful peace and happiness in their lives and in those of the women and men they formed relationships with.

Affirmation

I demand of myself that I become the man I came here to be. I easily free myself of limitations and access my true potential daily.

My tip for your path to peace

Define yourself by your own ideals of greatness and not by those of your culture. Freedom from imposed constraints promotes peace.

The essence

If every man is made in God's likeness, he therefore has the potential to be a 'god' on earth. It is simply a choice (made daily) as to what thoughts you think, the words you speak and the actions you take.

Being a goddess

ALL WOMEN HAVE A GODDESS WITHIN. HELP HER TO EMERGE AND SHINE.

Being a goddess is about embracing beauty within ourselves. It is how we present ourselves to the world in every moment. It could be beautiful words, beautiful deeds, beautiful surroundings or beautiful clothes, jewellery and lotions to adorn ourselves with. Beautifying our surroundings at work and at home keeps us inspired, creative and loving towards ourselves and others. It is about noticing beauty in the simplest of moments: an unexpected smile from a stranger or a compliment that elevates our self-worth.

Immerse yourself in nature whenever possible. Goddesses need to recharge in the sun—allow it to kiss your body. Nature abounds in simple moments of beauty whether it's bees in flight from flower to flower or waves crashing onto a beach. Connect with nature to access your inner goddess.

Being a goddess is about being you, the authentic you, and shining your light so that others are inspired to do the same. Embrace the power of you without 'modifying' yourself to please others.

Nurturing yourself and loving yourself is a must if you hope to be able to do this for others.

My tips for becoming a 'goddess' who owns her self-worth, power and beauty in all its many forms

> Make you and self-care a priority in your own life.
> Take a leap of faith and go in that direction you've always wanted to take.
> Find ways to discover your unique gifts and use them to make the world a better place.
> Discover some form of energy healing.
> Love as much and as often as you can.
> Learn to trust yourself and your intuition.
> Have gratitude for the smallest of things.
> Use your words wisely and kindly.
> Give up judgement of yourself.
> Use your thoughts creatively and positively.
> Stay in the present moment.
> Move your body.
> Relax, smile and laugh lots.
> Ask for universal guidance.
> Surround yourself with people and things that make you feel great.
> Go within and ask, what works for me? What is true for me?

Affirmation

I am a goddess who owns her self-worth, beauty and power in all its many forms.

> **My tip for your path to peace**
>
> Create your own definition of beauty and be that. Freedom from comparison with others is peace.

The essence

The experience of life is elevated through seeing and expressing beauty in all its forms. A goddess is born when she expresses gratitude, appreciates all that is hers, and moves through life with grace, compassion and dignity.

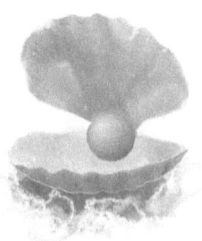

Being uncomfortable

BEING UNCOMFORTABLE MEANS THERE IS SOME SERIOUS LIGHT COMING FROM THE OTHER END OF THE RAINBOW.

Do you have a ceiling on what you can have in life? To challenge this 'ceiling' you need to become comfortable being uncomfortable. Our comfort zone is found in any area that doesn't challenge us to be any greater. It's also the areas within that we refuse to look at or acknowledge as we've decided it's too painful to go there. Being uncomfortable is a wonderful guide helping us to identify places within that require healing. It can be the areas of our lives and personal qualities that we numb ourselves from that we avoid looking at through addictive, distracting behaviours. We can become comfortable with limitations because it can feel safe and we don't have to risk failure or disappointment. Relish discomfort that is challenging you to move forward, to step up and to release old patterns of limited thinking.

Sometimes things must be uncomfortable enough to provide the necessary rocket fuel for the change that our spirit is demanding to come forth. We need to stretch ourselves in order to be surprised and amazed by ourselves and what we can achieve. We all have talents and abilities that remain hidden unless we take some risks and move in directions that encourage these abilities to come forth. Each time we step out of our comfort zone our confidence grows and we are more able and willing to shine our light.

The ego will most likely attempt to convince you to stay 'small and safe'. Your spirit, your true self, wants you to explore and soar, free of fear. From here you can say, 'Hello, new ways of seeing, believing and receiving more of the bounty life has to offer'.

Being uncomfortable is a great indicator that you are facing something (usually within) and that change is calling and is already on its way. Avoid resistance and you will emerge with greater flow and peace from this transition.

Being uncomfortable could be your potential calling, wanting to take you in new directions and to new places. You will feel niggles until you answer the call. Break free of resistance and procrastination and take a leap of faith. What is there to lose, other than limitation and mundane living?

Affirmation

*I seek ways to stretch my thinking and attitudes.
I stay alert and in a state of readiness
to access new opportunities and learning.*

My tip for your path to peace

Push yourself to move forward in small ways every day. Each risk you take stretches you, increases your confidence to embrace change, and takes you one step closer to realising new dreams. Peace lies in the greatness that can exist within us, beyond being uncomfortable.

The essence

We discover our true potential every time we take an inspired action, adopt a new attitude, change any thinking or response (that is outside our daily comfort zone), or embrace a different way of operating. New doors are opened leading to the discovery of hidden talents and abilities. Diamonds are made under pressure.

Being unstoppable

BEING UNSTOPPABLE IS A PROCESS AND A WAY OF BEING, NOT JUST A DESTINATION.

For us to be unstoppable we need to embrace physical, emotional and mental healing. Optimal health will provide a greater basis for us to utilise motivation and inspiration to create desired outcomes in life. Being persistent, having faith in ourselves and trusting in universal guidance enhances our chances of being unstoppable.

Our power and momentum will be tested through a range of conditions and experiences. Moments of self-doubt and insecurity can temporarily stop us in our tracks. Putting ourselves down through unhealthy comparison with others also hinders our progress. We will be tempted to give up through perceived failure—or even sometimes if our work isn't received in the way we have decided it should be.

When situations or 'individuals' arise to delay our ability to move forward, we need to pick ourselves up and keep going, trusting that every small step makes a difference. Delving into our self-care toolkit (which is anything that makes us reach for better-feeling emotions and thoughts and enhances our wellbeing) is essential for getting back on track if we have been derailed in any way.

Remember that failures are not really failures: they are opportunities to reflect, regroup or go in another direction, often for our highest good. As one door closes another swings wide open for us, if we are willing to notice it. Being in a state of alert awareness and receptivity (for things to occur in ways that we hadn't initially planned) is key. Surrender is an important element of being unstoppable. Being free of needing to control every outcome means we stay open to new possibilities as they arise.

Build the energy of 'unstoppability' by fuelling your motivation and inspiration. Set some goals or intentions that make you want to jump out of bed each morning and the next morning and the next. Inspiration makes magic happen. Hold wonderful visions for yourself and at the same time focus on what you already have; this creates the space for attracting more possibilities. Gratitude and appreciation are high vibration states that draw wonderful things into our lives.

Recognise that when we stand in our power and presence, we truly are unstoppable. No-one can stop or limit us in life: we are the only ones powerful enough to do that. Be the best coach that you can be for you and your life. Reach for the stars and who knows, you might find a whole new galaxy.

Affirmation

I freely look within to identify and release all perceived limitations to being unstoppable in life.

My tip for your path to peace

Recognise self-doubt and comparison as illusionary states that have no power over us. Commit to achieving your dreams (or something better) and enjoy the associated peace, contentment and success that arises with this approach.

The essence

Being unstoppable is a state of mind and an action stance that we need to embrace to successfully move through life with power and purpose.

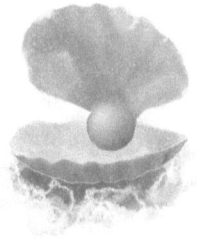

Body

LOVE YOUR BODY AND AS EACH CELL IS FUELLED WITH GREATER HEALING CAPACITY, IT WILL LOVE YOU RIGHT BACK.

Creating your ideal body involves more than eating less and exercising more. There are physical, dietary, hormonal and psychological factors that come into play. Endeavour to shine light on the self-beliefs, dietary habits and emotional and mental patterns standing in the way of your ideal body. Weight gain or weight loss requires a holistic approach. Attempt to tune into what your body needs. Ask it what it needs to heal or what it would take to shift excess weight. Connect to your intuition and truly listen. See what food or healing modalities you are drawn to.

Sensitive beings are affected by the energies of others and places. Be selective with whom and where you spend your time, thus protecting your energies. Develop your awareness of how your body responds to and is impacted by the energies of others. For me, the energies of others hit in the solar plexus area. When (and where) information lands in your body, breathe deeply to process and release the information before it impacts your body, thoughts and emotions. Learning to recognise what is yours (as opposed to something you've picked up) is essential for the health of sensitive, empathic types. Learn to manage your gifts so they are helpful in life, for you and others.

Pain and illness are our body's way of communicating with us. What is your body trying to tell you? What are you still holding onto, that you could be letting go of? Investigate the metaphysical causes, the emotional and mental underlying patterns of dis-ease, to shed light on what is really going on for you and your body. Identifying the emotional pattern, responding to it and releasing it helps the mind and body to heal before physical ailments show up.

Our bodies respond to the content of our thoughts. Louise Hay says that 'Dis-ease can be reversed by simply reversing mental patterns'. Each cell is affected by the energy associated with our thoughts and feelings. Program your body with high vibrational, healing thoughts. It will love you for it and work even harder to heal you and your life. A body free of negative judgements being directed at it is a happy body. Judgement is a low vibrational, very toxic 'weapon' that we should avoid using against our bodies.

Discover what is healing and nurturing for your body. Try a range of healing modalities until you find what works for your body, mind and spirit. Reiki and acupuncture are two of my favourites. Both stimulate the body's limitless potential for healing. They work with our energy systems to help clear blockages, limitations and stress, enhancing our immune system, wellbeing and healing capacity. Reiki helps to clear low vibrational energies, including fear, shame, anxiety, anger and guilt, before they can contribute to dis-ease in the body.

For me, integrating the powerful belief that 'My body and life are designed to heal me' has led to many synchronistic encounters with the right people, therapists, healers, doctors and life-changing information revealing itself for greater health and healing.

Fuel your body with healing foods. Fruit, vegetables, herbs and spices are nature's gift to our bodies for healing. Hydration is key for our body systems and organs to function efficiently.

Our bodies love to move. Discover what physical exercise lights your body up. Dancing is great for shifting stagnant energies. Yoga poses clear our energy centres and certain poses are designed to improve specific organ and body part functioning. Yoga helps us connect to our breath and still our minds. With any exercise, deep breathing immediately works on calming our nervous system. Swimming is great for cleansing our energetic body and many people connect to their intuition and creativity when their bodies are immersed in water.

Being in nature is soothing for our body and spirit. Walking barefoot and grounding our energies is highly therapeutic. Our spirit and moods lift when outside in the elements and the power of sunshine in healthy doses can never be underestimated.

Our bodies thrive on all forms of love, connection and intimacy. They love appreciation, gratitude and kindness. How can you gift love and nurturing to your body today?

Affirmation

*I release all judgements of my body.
I choose to see it as a miraculous
home for my beautiful spirit.
It supports me and heals me
twenty-four hours a day.*

My tip for your path to peace

A relaxed calm mind free of judgements directed at the body invokes feelings of wellbeing, self-worth and peace with what is.

The essence

Our bodies are miracles and they perform miracles every day. We need to honour, cherish and nurture them to maximise our health and wellbeing.

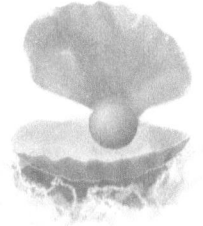

Books

A MIND THAT LEARNS, TEACHES.

Books are little treasures of wisdom just waiting to be opened, absorbed and assimilated. When we read, we relate to ourselves, others and life in general. There are always new perspectives, insight and knowledge to be gained within books.

Books are a gift as they take us straight to the now, the present moment. Through reading our mind is withdrawn from the past and future and captivated by the now. Our mind is beautifully and meaningfully absorbed by what is taking place between the covers of a book. Our day-to-day dilemmas become a distant hum as our minds visualise, predict, question, relate, integrate and become one with the story or teaching.

Books allow us to decipher our world as we learn through the pages in front of us. We become more open to possibilities and points of view that we may not have considered. Our control and armour can be cracked open as we are challenged to ponder and question. We experience new worlds and places through the pages of books.

My day is always geared towards creating not only writing time but also reading time. It is my form of therapy. I am honouring myself by doing what nurtures and nourishes my soul. I am also honouring life, as the more I learn the more I can teach others.

Books make no demands on us, they just give what we are willing to receive in mind, body and spirit.

Affirmation

I allow myself to discover the joy and growth that accompanies reading material that comforts, inspires and challenges me.

My tip for your path to peace

Books are peace as they calm us. They are a form of relaxing meditation as they quieten our thinking. Stress is diffused and peace arises as we are captivated by the learning or stories that unfold before us.

The essence

Books are wisdom. They are teachers and soul-soothers from the heavens. Peace within is possible every time you open a book. Go within as magical possibilities await.

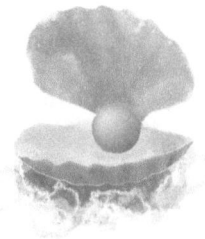

Bravery

BE THE LEADER OF YOUR LIFE,
TO LIVE AN INSPIRED LIFE.

Bravery is what is called for in these equally wondrous and tumultuous times. Bravery to find our voice, express our truth (and own it) and to follow what lights us up. The world needs more joy.

Each time one person steps up and insists on peace where there's conflict, compassion where there's indifference, and love where there's fear, we have a chance of bringing great change to our home, city, country and beautiful planet.

We need to be brave enough to truly care for ourselves so that we develop the self-worth, resilience and strength required to be leaders. This starts firstly with instigating changes that encourage greater peace in our own lives.

It's often easier to conform and to go with the majority because it makes fewer waves. However, moving away from the flock forges new direction, innovation and ways of seeing and perceiving. Creating your own reality means you get to live an inspired life that is perfectly designed for you and your needs.

The bravest act is looking within to find and free ourselves of anything that holds us back from reaching our greatest potential.

A sure-fire way to increase our level of courage is to be mindful of the stories we tell ourselves, as these stories shape our reality. We need to ensure that our stories lift us up rather than break us down.

Moving out of our comfort zone is another great way to develop bravery. Peace descends as we finally break free of resistance to what our spirit is calling for. True courage is being afraid of something but surging onwards despite it.

Affirmation

Bravery is my true nature. I allow it to take me where I need to go and free me of whatever needs to leave.

My tip for your path to peace

Don't resist the bravery that is arising within you waiting to be expressed. Peace prevails when there is no resistance.

The essence

The world needs us in our bravest states to bring about the change we desire for ourselves and the world.

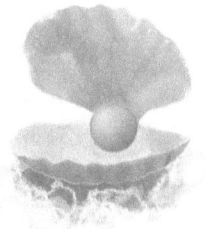

Chaos

A WAY FOR CRACKS TO OPEN
AND LIGHT TO FLOW IN.

When chaos descends, disrupting our lives, we often open to change, out of necessity. Coal under pressure creates diamonds, and we can also shine brightly after facing turbulence and challenge. Chaotic experiences are often catalysts for drawing on all that we are, to overcome obstacles and our own responses to them. Turbulence can make us step up even more and consequently has the effect of attracting in our desires, so that they manifest themselves at an even faster rate. When we have no control or answers, there is an opportunity for surrender. We can trust that the universe has our back and will guide us through any situation if we stay aligned with love, connect to our intuition, and release fear that stops us in our tracks. When we are truly tested, we need to embrace our faith, not our fear. It is easy to default to fear, as it is familiar. We need to make faith our natural response in order to truly thrive and shine.

During times of duress, we all have the power to manage our thoughts and corresponding emotional responses. Reach for better-feeling thoughts and emotions to reduce fear. Fear creates stress, which in turn creates inflammation and associated lowered immune function.

Out of chaos and suffering come possibilities for creation, greatness, renewal and beauty. Our suffering calls us to step up, as the old ways of functioning (from fear and control) no longer work. In times of chaos we need to take the time to pause (for a personal reset and review) and connect with our inner guidance. In times of unpredictability and upheaval we are often called to be and do many things that are unfamiliar to us: questioning habitual patterns; giving up control; managing our fear; and surrendering to our higher power. We are forced to dig deep and find solutions within, to effectively manage and change our outer conditions. The old ways generally don't offer the solutions we are seeking. Often a new pathway and approach will provide answers.

Some examples of chaos leading to creation and beauty:
- We may become terrified of contracting a disease and through this learn to focus on increasing wellbeing and having gratitude for the health we have today.
- We may be struck by an illness, recover and value life so much that we reach for the stars, manifesting new dreams.
- We may lose our job or business and find ourselves on a new pathway that is more aligned with who we are at a soul level, leading to a career beyond our wildest dreams.
- After suffering prolonged fear, we may finally appreciate that fear exacerbates problems. We may allow light and love to be our new leaders.

- With livelihoods taken or changed, we may find an even greater use for our gifts and talents, along with renewed purpose and meaning in life.
- An industry collapses and as a result, surrounding waterways become clear with fish and birdlife returning. Upon recommencement of production, the industry introduces new policies that support environmental health.
- Where people have a stance of maintaining separation from others, they may seek comfort and connection, discovering a new level of community and support.
- Loved ones and friendships that may have been taken for granted now become dear to us.
- Materialism and consumerism may give way to greater connection with others, simpler truths, values and new understanding.
- Our frantic, fast-paced lifestyles may give way to peaceful and more present ways of living and being.
- Our spiritual lives and pursuits (which many people are forced to access for the first time during a crisis) may be valued as much as our earthly lives and pursuits.
- And my most challenging, tumultuous time: losing my sight for three months (after a routine laser procedure to correct mild short-sightedness) and developing my 'sixth sense' and new life trajectory.

When outside circumstances are out of our control, we may be forced to look within and change what really matters—that is, anything that limits our ability to be the best version of ourselves.

Any kind of loss (both financial and personal) which often accompanies chaos, provides us with a choice: we can cling tightly to our old patterns, or we can allow ourselves to open to something new. We always have choice as to how we react and move forward. Comfort zones and good times often don't awaken us to new ways of seeing and functioning, but chaos most certainly will. We need to embrace disorder as a part of the creative process of life. To most effectively navigate chaotic times we need to spend our lives seeking connection with our highest good, stay in alignment with our higher selves, and make self-care our divine responsibility. With these high vibrational states in place we can then ebb and flow beautifully with the tides.

Affirmation

*I trust that I have the strength
and inner guidance available to
handle all that life presents.
I know that out of chaos comes new
possibilities for creation and
beauty to enter my life.*

My tip for your path to peace

Choose the thinking that takes you back to inner peace. Trust that this too shall pass into something better. Dive deeply into your self-care toolkit to fill your own cup with more peace. Rise above any storms and find your own version of sunshine.

The essence

Chaos forces us to lose control and to create from a new space, a space where we have surrendered to something greater than ourselves. On a personal and global level during chaotic, turbulent times our greatness, our light, is needed. Chaos provides us with an opportunity to practise transforming fear into faith. Listen to your inner wisdom and generate hope and positivity within. Solutions arise from new energy, thinking and functioning. The world changes one person at a time. Imagine and be the change you'd like to see in the world.

Circle

QUALITY ABOVE ALL ELSE, WHEN
INVITING PEOPLE INTO YOUR LIFE.

A circle could be defined as any group that we belong to on a social, work or family basis. The groups often demonstrate commonalities such as cultural ideals, values or coming together for a common purpose. These groups allow us opportunities to connect deeply, provide support and work towards achieving common goals. They can challenge us to be greater as the energy of a group helps us to step up. Positive energy on a large scale can work miracles. On the flip side groups can make us feel so safe and settled that we rarely step out of our comfort zones. Balance is key.

There are no rules within circles and the members and situations can change throughout our lives as we evolve and attract into our world exactly what we need. It is important to allow flow in our circles. As some people naturally drift from our lives the space is made for new people to arrive who very often support and nurture where we are currently at.

Many people on the spiritual path to claiming and being all of themselves can become a little lonely as friends that no longer resonate with them drift away. When we radiate inner peace and joy, it can be very challenging for those who are more committed to staying unhappy than seeking change. Becoming too happy and stepping up too far can make some friends feel uncomfortable if they are not ready for change. Change is overwhelming for those who are not quite ready for it. Your vibe and clarity may be too strong and unsettling for some—enter resistance and possibly judgement. People will change in their own time, or not. Confidence, presence and authenticity can be intimidating for those who have not yet recognised or embraced those qualities within themselves. Not everyone will be willing to go where you are going and that is okay. You are more than enough and always will be.

If people leave your life, there is space for those with a similar vibe and energy to come into your life, as like often attracts like. Your new connections will be based on greater authenticity, which is lighter and way more fun. Trust that your new circle is on its way. Your new circle members also have work to do before they are ready to connect with you.

It is important to release feelings of loneliness and abandonment if you don't connect regularly with a circle. Look for connections in all your days in all situations. Stay open to receive. Surprise encounters are a universal specialty. Trust that you are calling into your world exactly who you truly require—that is, people who will resonate with who you are, and will assist you to create a life that brings you peace and joy.

Affirmation

I trust that the people I require for love, support and guidance show up in my life at just the right times. I am loved, and I belong.

My tip for your path to peace

Be content with and grateful for those people that are showing up in your life. Being in allowance of the current 'status' of your circle will bring you greater peace.

What contribution can you be to foster even deeper, peaceful and more joyful connections?

The essence

Allow flow with your circle. Your circles may change throughout your life to suit where you're at, or you may resonate with the same crew throughout your life. All is good with either scenario if you are honoured, supported and feel good being in the company of your circle members. Trust your intuition. If they are not your vibe, they may not be your tribe.

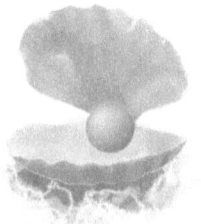

Comparison

DON'T COMPARE YOUR LIFE TO OTHERS, THEIR JOURNEY IS UNIQUELY DESIGNED FOR THEM, AS IS YOURS.

Comparison is crippling for many. Unless your self-worth is untouchable, avoid the comparison trap. Don't compare the chapters in your story to anyone else's, as their life and the accompanying lessons and highlights are purely for them. Comparison (which always involves judgement directed either at self or at others) lowers our vibration. It does not come from a state of love, and as such is a lower energy state.

If comparison is an issue you are currently working through, resist looking at what people are doing on Facebook. Seek to be the authentic version of you, not a replica of what someone else is doing, being or creating. The Facebook world is often one of illusion. Many people tend to post how they would like their lives to be perceived, rather than the actual reality. Facebook can be also be another form of escapism and addiction, a means to distract oneself from what is really going on. Avoid the need for the validation, attention and acknowledgement that can become addictive in this arena. Be very discerning with your use of social media.

Remember the old adage, 'what other people think of you is none of your business'. This can be a very helpful stance to take if you are in the public eye or putting your work and opinions out into the world. Focus on your message, your work and its authenticity. If you are proud of your work, own it. Avoid being limited by the opinions of others regarding you or your work. Constructive feedback is useful, but criticism designed to limit and undermine you is not okay.

There are a lot of people out there doing amazing things. We need to allow them to inspire us without focusing so much on their amazingness that we forget to cultivate and nurture our own. Seeing the amazingness of someone else is often a sign that we also possess that quality—we just haven't yet acknowledged or cultivated it, but it's on its way.

The potential for self-doubt and inaction is a risk associated with comparison. Being your most wonderful, authentic self is where the magic happens. It is not in trying to compare yourself to others and then adjusting yourself accordingly.

Affirmations

Each day I go within, connect with my intuitive self and identify that which is great about me. I focus my attention on the steps I am taking to create my desired reality.

There is no-one else like me. I have a pathway and a destiny that is being crafted uniquely for me - for a life beyond my wildest dreams.

My tip for your path to peace

Focus all your energy and attention on the contribution you are making to your own life and that of others. This creates the space for peace to prevail as you are content with the way you are showing up in your own life.

The essence

There are a lot of people out there doing fantastic stuff. Don't get caught in the comparison trap as it will dull your sparkle, contribute to self-doubt and limit your creativity. Allow others to inspire you, but focus on your own amazingness and authentic self. That's where you get to discover your true potential.

Compassion

ACCESS COMPASSION AND YOU ACCESS THE DIVINE.

Compassion is suspending our judgements and thought processes long enough to put ourselves in someone else's shoes and at the same time extending love and understanding to what they are saying and experiencing. It's putting our ego aside and accessing our higher self and bringing this to the present moment. Compassion can have an almost magical way of easing the suffering around us.

Bringing compassion to all our connections and relationships has the power to change and elevate all that is, in that moment. From this space miracles arise in ourselves and others. We have the potential to say just what the person needs to hear for healing, forgiveness, moving forward, changing, growing or making inspired choices.

It is equally important to extend compassion to ourselves. As we forgive, nurture and treat ourselves with kindness and respect we are being compassionate. Leaning towards compassion for ourselves builds self-worth and strength. We can more successfully navigate life from a place of compassion. The spirit of compassion gives us the closest possible connection to divine energies and raises our own level of consciousness. We bring heaven one step closer to earth.

Affirmation

I allow my true essence, my compassionate self to arise freely to enhance my growth and that of others.

My tip for your path to peace

Quiet your mind, suspend judgement and be so present with another that you truly listen (without waiting for your turn to speak) and receive the peace, love and potential for transformation that exists in this space. Compassion for self brings inner peace as we release self-judgement and enhance our self-worth.

The essence

Compassion is applying love and understanding to situations and relationships to bring out the best in others and in oneself. Compassion gives others the gift of peace. It soothes souls. It enhances love in all our relationships.

Competition

GET FREE OF THE PROGRAM AND
LIVE YOUR BEST LIFE … IN PEACE.

Competition seems to have been programmed into us very early in life (via the ego) as a misaligned attempt to convince us that survival of the fittest, smartest, wealthiest, most beautiful and most successful (to name but a few examples) is essential. This approach limits the peace we can experience in life as there is an element of never having or being enough. It can also be extremely expensive if there is an associated need to always be seen having or doing the best, latest and greatest.

Women throughout the ages have known instinctively that to survive in the harshest of environments (and at various times throughout history), aligning ourselves with the most powerful men is a matter of survival and 'thrival'. How was this done? Often through 'peacocking': being the most beautiful, well-dressed and sensual woman around. Women were also compelled to present whatever body shape was desired for that time in history.

Unfortunately, there is a hangover from this approach. For many women this has resulted today in the need to cut, fill and inject bodies and faces with any number of dubious products. In this process women have set themselves up to 'never be quite good enough' and often look for the next procedure or diet to compete with what society projects as the current ideal. Energy and time is then taken away from more meaningful life-enhancing pursuits and from cultivating inner beauty.

Many women today can feel uncomfortable or intimidated around beautiful women. This creates separation rather than connection. We need to remember that beauty comes in all forms, that there is enough to go around, and that when it shines from within there is no denying it. When we can appreciate beauty in others, we can also have it as our own perception of self. Before long, if we consistently stay in this space, we can see and appreciate our own beauty.

Feeling ourselves being drawn into a place of competition provides a great opportunity to take steps to be free of the ego. Feelings of jealousy, envy, comparison and competition are all signs that we are in the grips of the ego, rather than radiating the presence of our true selves. Us as beings know in our hearts that there is enough of everything to go around.

As spiritual beings having an earthly experience, we are so aware (even when unacknowledged) that when we respond in competitive ways to others on superficial matters, we create feelings of unease within. These feelings show us that it is not in our best interest to give in to negative emotional states (and corresponding thought patterns) if we wish to live a life of peace.

When competitive jealousy is directed at you, see it for what it is: an attempt at separation. Remember to look past smoke screens and illusions. Ask 'What am I truly seeing here?' and 'What is the truth under this?' Avoid dimming your own light or being less than your authentic self in order to make others feel more comfortable around you. It is their issue to work through and grow from. Avoid validating the experience for them by attempting to play small or become less visible.

Avoid falling into the trap of thinking if it's been done before, or someone else has it, it's not for you. We each have a unique contribution to make. Celebrate the successes of others to raise your vibration and open your own door to more receiving. Jealousy and competition are blocks to magic and possibility flowing into our lives. Think of brides and weddings: each bride and the way she presents her wedding to the world is uniquely beautiful. Each one lights up the world around her in their own way. We need more of that.

Affirmations

I don't need to compete as I am complete.

I choose to be disconnected from the
'female survival through competition collective'.
I no longer choose to be a part of this program.
I cut all energetic ties connecting me to it
and now see through eyes of love.

My tip for your path to peace

Believe in your heart that there is an abundance of everything we desire, for us all. Peace comes when we release competition and trust that if someone else is doing it or having it, so can we, in our own way, in our time.

The essence

Competition implies that we are 'less than', and this is never true. We are all equal, just on different paths with attributes unique to us. When we are comfortable in our own skin, aligned with our higher self and truly thriving, we can be free of the detrimental effects of competition. Acknowledging the areas in our lives where we compete to separate allows us to learn a lot about ourselves (and others) as we move forwards along the path of peace and awareness.

Compliments

COMPLIMENTS ARE LITTLE SPARKS OF MIRACLE DUST.

Genuine, meaningful compliments are gifts to our self-worth as they can change in a heartbeat how we currently feel about ourselves. Compliments over time build feelings of worth and esteem. They awaken us to seeing ourselves in a new light. Sometimes all it takes to change our perceptions of self is to witness ourselves through the eyes and expressions of another. Compliments are the weapons of a light worker. Help others to focus on the positives, as it is all too easy to focus on flaws. Every small shift in perception and worth opens doors for greater worth. Each compliment given or received is a miracle as it instantly elevates mood and energy.

Compliments provide an instant hit of joy. After each 'hit', we vibrate at a frequency higher than that existing prior to the compliment. For anyone that is feeling a little flat, a compliment can lift them to optimism and happiness, for in that moment they are distracted from past or future pondering and are in the now, where all is well. Compliments force us into the present moment, where our true power lies.

Compliments are gifts to the recipient and to the generous person who has bestowed them. As we give a compliment, we are sending love. Sending love raises our own vibration and contributes to our feelings of wellbeing. Experiencing someone respond to a heartfelt compliment is such a joy. It is magical as there is always an unpredictable ripple effect.

Have enormous gratitude for compliments and receive them graciously. The more love and appreciation we have for ourselves, the more we draw in compliments. When we are feeling great about ourselves, others cannot help but see our light and compliments flow in more frequently.

While cherishing unexpected compliments, spend as much time as you can inwardly complimenting yourself. Build your own vibration. Like attracts like and compliments attract more of the same. Never rely on compliments for your worth; you are always enough. See them as miracle gifts to be treasured. Pay them forward in genuine ways as much as possible. Let's change the world one compliment at a time.

Affirmation

*Today is a day to embrace the
power of compliments.
They come to me from expected
and unexpected sources.
I am aware and alert for opportunities
to lift the spirit of myself and others
with my beautiful words.*

My tip for your path to peace

Compliments promote peace as they are surrounded by an aura of 'all is well'. I have a little section in the notes in my phone, my own 'feelings of peace vault.' In it I record beautiful compliments that have inspired, calmed and nurtured me. I draw on this during times where I need greater peace and contentment.

The essence

Compliments are powerful tools for transformation. They open our eyes to our true, highest nature and give others new ways of perceiving themselves.

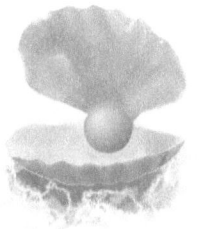

Connections

THE GREATEST TEACHERS,
WHO TAKE US TO NEW PLACES.

Our connections with others truly help us discover who we are and how we function. Some of our most challenging connections provide the greatest source of change and insight. These angels in disguise are mirrors shining light on those parts of ourselves we may not have been willing to see. Why do we react to that person the way we do? What judgement of ourselves do we have in relation to that person? What qualities do I loathe or adore in that person—qualities that I also have? What is it that our ego desires that we don't see?

Cherish those amazing souls that inspire us to choose more greatness than we are currently willing to have, just by their presence and the example of living they demonstrate. Anywhere there is love in our connections there is more opportunity to grow and change. Love is a high vibrational state and will always help us attract what we require and desire.

Be seen, be amongst it. Avoid separating yourself from others as a misguided way to stay safe. Isolating ourselves can keep us small and take away the opportunities and steps required to create the lives we're truly destined for. At the same time be discerning as to who you spend your time with—your spirit knows who and what will serve it well. Value your time alone also, as this can recharge us and make us receptive to connecting with others.

People often come into our lives at just the right time to give us messages and encourage the growth needed to keep our lives moving forward. Be open to coincidences and synchronicity.

Affirmation

I allow my connections to reveal with ease what is required for my growth and healing.

My tip for your path to peace

When reactions arise during engagement with others, stop, breathe and centre yourself. From this space of greater peace ask to be shown what it is you need to perceive and receive. With clarity comes opportunities for peace.

The essence

People provide the greatest mirrors for us to see our limitations and potential. Stay aware and present during all your encounters for the greatest learning about self.

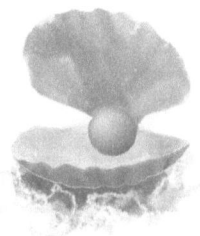

Consuming

RECEIVE FROM THE WORLD THAT WHICH NOURISHES YOU, RATHER THAN BEING CONSUMED BY NEEDS.

How does one move from being a merciless consumer to a mindful consumer? The answer is to truly know thyself and thy motivations. For me, mindless consuming generally distracts me from what I am resisting. Often this is my creativity, the call to write. I used to beautifully express my creativity with a myriad of beautifully put-together outfits. The hit of this type of creativity was there but it wasn't enduring or satisfying. Before consuming, we need to reflect on what we may be distracting ourselves from, to determine what need is being served.

When choosing to become mindful consumers we put our ego on the backburner as we are not allowing it to convince us that we need this or need that. We take charge of our lives and create more space for new possibilities and potential to show up, as we are not being distracted by 'consuming'.

Plan on viewing, eating and drinking what nourishes you, and only buy truly beautiful or essential items. During the transition process (and it can be lengthy) from mindless to mindful consuming, be kind to yourself whenever you slip up. It often takes many failed attempts to form new positive habits, which means the failed attempts are really successes in disguise.

Indulgence for me is now also about time, rather than consuming: time to spend doing what I love, being where I love and with those I love.

By the way, if you have regular energy healing work, you become less inclined to do things that don't nourish you physically, mentally and emotionally, as you step more into a space that supports all aspects of your wellbeing.

Affirmation
*I follow what lights me up
and mindfully consume
what the world has to offer,
for my highest good.*

My tip for your path to peace

Greater peace can come with mindful consuming as we've broken the 'want, have, want, have' cycle and possible associated guilt. Celebrate success and be kind when regressing. Peace comes from total acceptance of where we are at, and from trusting that we will move forward in our own time.

The essence

Know yourself. Wisdom is freedom and power. It is enlightening to fully understand why we are consuming (and what we are consuming), whether it is in the form of material goods, food, alcohol or social media.

Contrasts

CONTRASTS ARE CATALYSTS FOR
MOVEMENT, CHANGE,
AND GROWTH.

Life is abundant in contrasts and is not always a bed of roses. Contrasts move us forward in life. Out of suffering comes greatness as we step up in order to meet new challenges in ways we couldn't have imagined. Accept 'what is' and at the same time embrace 'this too shall pass'. Trust deeply that each stage has its day and will eventually shift. New horizons await and we need to be ready for them.

Contrasts help us to grow and to appreciate the good times even more. Without a 'disastrous' relationship, we may not appreciate harmony and unconditional love to the same degree. Without the experience of ill health, we may not have respect for the amazing capacity of our bodies to heal. Without chaos and stress, we may not appreciate calm. Weekends seem even more amazing after our working weeks come to an end. Landing a dream job that lights us up seems even more wonderful and miraculous after having a job that has consumed our life or impacted our health. Living in an old home and then putting in our own touches (through renovations and improvements) brings such home pride and peace. Cooking for a family and then being on holiday and having someone else cook and clean is a heavenly contrast. Indulging in our favourite (and sometimes unhealthy) foods makes the healthier choices a real standout. Children and family members who have had emotional struggles or hardship and who then experience success or change allow sadness to be replaced with joy and gratitude.

Nature abounds in evidence of the power of contrasts. Without winter we may not appreciate balmy summer nights. What joy spring flowers bring after the bare, stark trees of winter. We adore sunny days and blue skies after bleak days.

Life only gives us what we can handle. Embrace all of it and allow it to stretch and move you forward in unexpected and often synchronistic ways.

Affirmation

*I welcome contrasts in my life.
They show me what I truly want and
need to move towards a life of
peace and contentment.*

My tip for your path to peace

Be grateful for all the contrasts in life. We experience moments of peace and elements of pure joy as we appreciate what is, after a challenging 'contrast'.

The essence

Embracing and appreciating all the contrasts in our lives provides us with opportunities for personal growth. We know we are truly alive through the experience of contrasts.

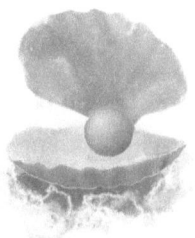

Creativity

CREATIVITY IS WORK THAT LIGHTS US UP FROM WITHIN, IT INSPIRES OUR HEART AND OFTEN COMES FROM A SOURCE OUTSIDE US.

Creativity makes me feel present, grounded and alive like nothing else can. The ego is quiet as I'm too focused to entertain it. There is calm. I feel aligned with the heavens and my muses and I are proud of the work we're creating. Creativity equals peace and freedom from anxiety, as I'm not resisting doing the work I'm called to do. As I write I am reminded of my own truths and at the same time I process and get free of my own stuff. Creativity moves our focus away from our problems and connects us with the power and potential available in the present moment. Creativity and the ability to produce something meaningful and worthwhile are wonderful for our self-worth and wellbeing. We are unlimited in our potential to create. When we choose to bring something new into our world, we tap into our content, purposeful, inspired and peaceful selves. Creativity connects us with our vitality, our life force. We can't control much of what happens in life, but we can always create which is a meaningful, proactive use of our energy.

Don't limit yourself, your life and the impact your work can have on others by keeping it all to yourself. Once you've done the work, put your creations out there. Detach from being vested in certain outcomes and allow your work to grow wings and go where it needs to go.

Make beautiful spaces, have personal rituals and peaceful settings for your creative work. This will assist you to connect with your muses and to truly listen. Open to them and be inspired and in awe of what comes through you. Everything else in my life flows better when I answer the call to write. There is a level of joy associated with writing that contributes to all that exists around me. I am living an inspired life venturing daily into the magic of the unknown.

Remember that even our thoughts are a form of creation. Fill your days with creative, expansive and positive thoughts that enhance your work and your life.

Affirmation

*I live an inspired life.
I am open to allowing creative inspiration
to flow through me with ease.*

My tip for your path to peace

Do the work you are drawn to create without resistance, so that peace and possibility can prevail in your life.

The essence

Creativity is inspired living. We embrace the mystery of the unknown and flow with divine energies. We connect with muses and information beyond what our human minds can conjure to create work that uplifts and inspires.

Declutter

IF IT DOESN'T NOURISH YOUR SPIRIT OR ENHANCE YOUR LIFE, PART WITH IT.

Decluttering our surroundings and possessions is so much better for us than we often acknowledge. Minimalism and simplicity bring greater peace to our lives and calm the mind. There is a correlation between letting go of our physical clutter and feeling calmer within. With more stillness in the mind, doors can open for new inspiration and creativity to flow in.

All objects and possessions have an energy or a memory associated with them. If it no longer lights you up when you gaze upon it, or it's not extremely useful … thank it for the time you spent together and send it on with love to someone else who might gain pleasure from it. Giving things away helps us to connect with our generous selves. What we let go of can then create a vacuum for drawing in something greater.

Letting go of things that don't bring us joy helps us to be free of the past and more present in today. As a part of decluttering and letting go, take a close look at your relationships. Do the people in your life still nurture you and bring the best out in you?

Work also on decluttering your mind. Do an inventory of the old stories and thought patterns that continually play out in your mind. Where attention goes, energy flows. Forgive yourself and others to create freedom from the limiting energy of resentment. Keeping our stuff keeps us trapped in a way of being and living that may no longer serve us or allow us to access our true potential.

Affirmation

*Let go, let go, let go.
I let go of all that no longer serves me
or lights me up, with ease.*

My tip for your path to peace

Look closely at your surroundings, both at work and at home. Feel the peace and space as you let go of 'clutter' that is no longer necessary for supporting you and your life. Look around and appreciate the clear energy. Allow this to spread to your mind, body and spirit.

The essence

Clearing physically clears you mentally. Feel the freedom as you make way for better things. Make the space for what is more in alignment with who you really are and with the life you'd like to create, to flow in.

Dreams

YOUR BELIEF GIVES THEM WINGS.

Dreams are living within you waiting to be realised and activated by you. Avoid the distractions, procrastination and self-doubt that separate you from your dreams. Self-doubt (although useful in keeping you alert to what's going on within) needs to be firmly placed in the far recesses of that huge 'Planet Mind'. Without second-guessing ourselves, much space is then available for inspiration and creativity to flourish. Consistently follow what brings you joy. Joy is the guiding light showing us the direction required for creating the life we came here to live. Hope keeps our dreams alive: allow it to flourish.

We are limited by our imaginations, but thankfully for us, the universe is not. The universe is vast, infinite and available for miracles when we can receive them. When putting your dreams and desires out into the universe, be expansive in your thinking. Let go control of outcomes and trust that the universe is on your side and will always be willing to go one bigger. For every step you take, the universe will take many more.

Feel deeply the joy and light that you intend to experience when your dreams become reality. From this space things manifest with greater ease. Elevated emotions, combined with the power of our positive thinking, are miracle workers. Make putting possibilities and questions out into the universe a daily practice. Then give your desires wings; let them go and allow time for the universe to work its magic. Give up being vested in outcomes. Be vigilant, listen for guidance, observe and connect with your intuition to know the steps required to make your dreams a reality. Strike when situations, events or people show up that match the energy of what you're trying to create. The dreams that truly serve our highest good will come true—or open the door for something even better to show up for us.

To support our dreams, we need to do the inner work. Our thoughts and emotions need to be aligned with our desires. Our faith needs to be greater than our fear and we need to trust that where we are going is better than where we have been. Back yourself and believe in yourself fully, or others may not; individuals pick up on the energetic messages we are broadcasting. Commit to taking intuitive action, combined with gratitude, appreciation and kindness to build momentum and power behind your dreams.

Affirmation

I send my dreams out into the universe
and freely hear divine guidance
to bring them to fruition.

> **My tip for your path to peace**
>
> Start each day by thinking about what currently brings you joy to build the energy of joy. Then stretch your thinking and imagine things you've deemed as impossible coming to fruition. Feel the energy and peace associated with believing these imaginings are already on the way.

The essence

Your dreams will become reality when your belief in them (and associated feelings) are greater than and far outweigh your feelings of doubt.

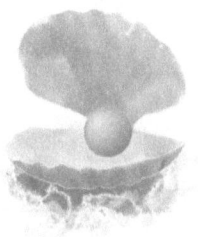

Ego

REFUSE TO ALLOW YOUR EGO TO
LEAD YOU AWAY FROM LOVE OR
LIMIT YOUR POTENTIAL.

The ego can be very basically described as the part of the mind that separates us from others or creates our sense of self-importance. Both are limitations to connecting with our true self. The ego is based on controlling rather than receiving and thrives on limiting us through fear.

The ego is adept at creating problems where there are none. It likes to take us away from love, forgiveness, creativity and possibility, and into fear and limitation. If it takes over your thinking it results in drama, grievances, reactivity, self-doubt, blaming, incessant wanting and envy. It encourages us to rely on validation from others, rather than trusting ourselves. The ego is like a virus that keeps us living in our head, creating worst-case scenarios.

The survival of the ego is paramount and therefore it always needs to be right, as being wrong is hugely threatening. The ego takes us way from the power of now as it wants us to focus on the future or dwell on the past, rather than the present moment.

The unkind, judgemental voice is the ego. It encourages us to compare ourselves to others through judgement and the resulting feelings of superiority or inferiority. Inevitably it wins with any form of judgement, as it takes us away from seeing the truth that we are all equal.

There is an alternative! Learn to identify the false beliefs that make up your ego. This will support you in listening to your true self and being guided by your intuition. Catch the ego at work as soon as possible and redirect your thinking. Meditation and energetic healing help us to quiet the mind in order to go beyond the ego and discover our true selves and the unlimited potential that lies within. When the ego quietens, we get to be everything we are, way beyond anything the ego can create. We connect to our heart space and our higher selves when the ego is diminished.

Affirmation

I choose to instantly reframe negative thinking into positive as I immediately recognise it as the voice of the ego.

My tip for your path to peace

Work on finding your worth every minute of every day. Healthy self-worth means peace is your natural ally and default position. You are always good enough. Ignore the voice that tells you anything less. The ego is terrified that you will shine so brightly that it will be totally eclipsed.

The essence

The ego is always looking for ways for us to perceive faults in ourselves and others to keep us in a state of unease and limitation. It is threatened by our growth and knows it 'dies' when we stop listening to the mean voice and step into shining our power and light.

Embarrassing moments

LEARN TO LAUGH AT YOURSELF ...
AND WATCH THE EXPLOSION OF JOY
AND HUMOUR THAT ARISES FOR ALL
AROUND.

The impact of embarrassing moments often comes down to our points of view, our judgement and self-esteem. These factors determine whether we want to disappear into the ground or laugh hysterically.

I've always found embarrassing moments a great way to bond with others over shared hysteria and joy. These moments can also give us a little insight into how well developed our self-worth is. If we can laugh at ourselves, we have a great relationship with our self-worth.

If we engage in stressing over what others may think of us, there's work to be done in the self-worth department. I've found the saying 'what other people think of me is none of my business' quite liberating during times of borderline extreme embarrassment. It helps me to step into finding the funnier side of things.

My children learned from me the gift of laughing at oneself the day I fell asleep while sunbaking on the beach in a bikini.

When I awoke on my sun lounger, my teenage children had abandoned me, and I found myself with a wedding taking place only metres away. The guests had trailed past and let me be, and obviously so had my children—so quickly that they hadn't warned me!

I'm sure I'm not the only woman to have had the skirt-tucked-into-the-pants scenario. I walked out on duty like this one day because the teachers who had witnessed me walking by thought it was one of the new fashionable uneven hemlines—very uneven and very unfashionable! The laughter among the staff who knew what was really going on created joy in the school that day. It also reminded us teachers that we don't have to be perfect models of exemplary standards every day!

Some of my fondest school memories are centred around embarrassing moments. In a memorable day in sewing class, I managed to cross-stitch the apron I was working on to my school dress. I'm sure the hysteria among my school friends lasted for days. The teacher was in tears of laughter, and we had a laugh at said incident thirty years later upon meeting again. It was a first for her!

Affirmation

*I cherish opportunities to laugh at myself
in a loving way. I love all my quirks.
Embarrassing moments provide me with
surprise opportunities for liberating
and joyful laughter.*

> **My tip for your path to peace**
>
> It's peaceful to be ourselves. Be yourself in all moments, even in the traditionally 'embarrassing' ones. Being comfortable in your own skin allows you to be at peace with whatever life presents.

The essence

Cherish the embarrassing moments as they provide lasting memories and points of connection with others through the joy of laughter.

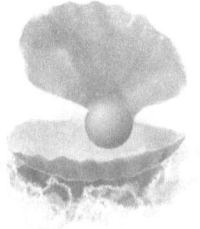

Emotions

FACE THEM, FEEL THEM,
FREE THEM.

If we are not feeling at peace emotionally then we have reacted to something, judged someone (or something), then judged ourselves for the judgement. It's a head-spinner, but that's how judgement works! We may also have taken on something from someone else, particularly if we are highly sensitive or empathic.

There is also the possibility that your body may be attempting to garner your attention in order to process some unresolved emotions. You may be at last releasing something that you have held onto for a long time. This is cause for celebration. If we don't listen to what our emotions are attempting to convey and work to release them, they can remain in the body causing dis-ease and physical ailments, which is a further way of getting our attention. There is wisdom for us in our emotions. For example, anger is often an unexpressed hurt or a need we have that is not being met. We need to feel our emotions, to get the message of learning that they have for us and move on. Don't allow them to linger and have any more power or airplay than is necessary.

Peace arises when we acknowledge and express our feelings. We can't experience peace as our background emotion unless we've faced certain emotions and healed the wounds underneath them. Once we've identified where we are at emotionally, we can redirect our thoughts and reach for better-feeling emotions, one emotion and thought at a time.

Be aware of not using distractions that can show up in the form of addictions (sugar, shopping, alcohol, social media use and so on) to avoid looking at your emotions.

Affirmation

*I cherish my emotions as the
loving messengers they truly be.
I sit with them.
I shine the light of my consciousness
on each emotion as they arise,
to perceive the gifts of truth
they are presenting.*

My tip for your path to peace

Consistently being aware of our emotions and the triggers and messages underneath them helps to move us effortlessly forwards on our healing journey. We move closer to peace as our emotions no longer define or limit us; they guide us.

The essence

The willingness to feel our emotions (and to then look within to discern their messages) creates the freedom for us to grow into the version of ourselves that is free of limitations. There are beautiful emotions to experience beyond the challenging ones.

Energy

IT IS EVERYWHERE, ACKNOWLEDGE IT AND EMBRACE IT.

Energy is the often mysterious and hard-to-grasp force behind all that exists in the universe. It is what everything is made from. It's invisible but available in every moment. It is the force that holds and brings into existence our thoughts, ideas and desires. When we tune into that energetic spark within us, we immediately connect to our intuition, healing capacity, talents and abilities, creativity and divine connection.

We have been blessed with four bodies: our physical body, our emotional body, our intellectual body and our energetic body. True healing occurs when all four bodies are balanced and clear. Our energies filter what we are willing to give out into the world and also determine what we are willing to receive. If we are taking care of our energetic bodies, we will feel energised rather than drained. We won't need artificial stimulants and we will have the energy to create.

Protect your energetic boundaries, that invisible force that surrounds you. If we are confident, present, healthy (alcohol and drugs can cause holes in our boundaries), trusting in life and standing in our power, then we create strong boundaries.

We strengthen our boundaries when we are clear on what is acceptable and unacceptable for us. Learn to say 'no' and be selective about where and with whom you spend your time. Be aware of those that drain your energy. Avoid taking on things for others. If we aren't feeling peace within, there's a fair chance we may have taken on something from someone else. Learn to discern what is yours versus what you may have taken on from others.

Our emotional health and boundaries grow in strength when we cease to validate the lower vibrational energies of others by experiencing what they are experiencing. Asking the following questions has greatly assisted me to determine what is mine and what are energetic projections from others: 'What is real here?' and 'What is the truth?'

Return what you've taken on from others to the rightful owner's higher self. It may feel kind to take on things for others, but it can rob them of their own opportunities for growth. Many people change through hardship. Allow them to work on their own issues to move forward in life. Be empathetic rather than sympathetic. Acknowledge what's going on for them and empower them by asking what steps they can take to heal. This approach fosters strong boundaries in all parties.

There are many things we can do to enhance our energetic system. Balance your energy systems regularly through reiki, acupuncture or kinesiology. Epsom salts baths and ocean swims help to clear our energies. Imagining yourself surrounded in shiny, metallic silver can deflect negative energies away from your energy field. Crystals such as black tourmaline, haematite and black onyx have been reputed to protect our energies. Walk barefoot daily on the grass or hug a tree to ground and centre your energies. Grounding has been shown to have amazing health benefits, including reducing stress, increasing energy, relieving jetlag, lowering inflammation, promoting healing, reducing the effects of electromagnetic energy and improving sleep.

Breathe deeply to shift stagnant energies and old hurts. It only takes three cycles of deep breathing to calm the nervous system. Breathing deeply around someone who is draining you helps to lessen their impact. Pull your energies back from all over the universe (through divine white light) back into your space and into your body, to fuel the flames of your life. Surround yourself in a divine, white light bubble of protection. Stand in your presence and feel the power and love within and surrounding you to provide a beautiful deflective space for outside forces that may drain you. Pull your aura in closer so it is not merging as readily with the energy fields of others. I imagine a candle flame flickering strongly within to lessen the impact of what is happening around me. Bless any space that you enter with light and love before entering.

Reading the energy of a situation and listening to the energy behind someone's words is the key to connecting with and enhancing our intuition. This approach also protects our energies as we more readily perceive that which is not ours.

Despite everything we do, it is not always possible to deflect the negative energies of others. I find it particularly challenging when around family members, colleagues or friends who whinge, moan and complain about all the things not going right in their lives. It is not easy to get up and walk away from these situations as there is often the expectation that we connect and keep the peace. When someone is complaining it is hard not to join them as we often feel disconnected from them or unkind if we don't align with what they are saying. Often attempts to redirect the line of conversation can be perceived as not caring or a form of disengagement. It is also very easy to judge ourselves as not being 'sensitive' to where others are at. I have also made the mistake of trying to make myself less than or even made up a few 'troubles' of my own in order to make others feel better. This is not a good approach as we then divorce who we are and lower our own vibration by going to this place. Be who you are and attempt to raise the vibration of conversations. Avoid buying into someone's 'poor me' drama or story; where possible help them to gently change their perspective. Observe rather than react to what is being said and most importantly release the temptation to align with or take on what another is experiencing. All we can do in these situations is have a strong toolkit of strategies for managing these interactions and clearing our energies afterwards.

Affirmation

*I have clear, strong boundaries.
In every moment I am committed
to protecting my boundaries.*

My tip for your path to peace

Allow peace to flood your body as you ground your energies. Walk barefoot and imagine roots travelling from your feet deep into the earth's core. Stand in your presence and perceive your energetic strength. There is peace within our power.

The essence

Taking care of our energies helps us to create a peaceful, wise and healthy existence. We connect to our intuition and connect more fully with the best version of ourselves.

Envy

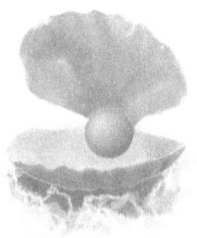

A LIGHTHOUSE FOR SHOWING US THE WAY TO OUR DESIRES.

Envy is a very dense and uncomfortable emotion. It comes with a sensation of despair and low self-worth. Envy (and its associated energy) implies that what we truly desire is either currently out of our reach or impossible, due to the inconvenient assumption (which may or may not be true) that someone else is already doing what we would like to be doing, or having the cake that we would like to have. Envy can fuel feelings of self-doubt, as seeing someone achieve that which we desire can trigger feelings of inadequacy. Envy can also be resistance to what is coming for us as we use the excuse that it's already been done, so it can't be done again. We need to remember that each person brings their own unique approach, flair, creativity and voice to any endeavour. We are all connected to the same universal intelligence, so there will always be many versions of a similar idea or approach. It hasn't been done before, because we haven't done it in our way, with our wisdom, gifts and abilities.

Jealousy pushes us further away from what we desire as it has a negative energy that can stop or interrupt our flow. It is a low vibrational state, and as a result, wonderful things will more than likely be repelled from, rather than drawn into, our lives. Turn jealousy into generosity of spirit to perfectly set the stage (energy) for attracting what you desire and require. Celebrating the successes of others raises our vibration and attracts great things into our lives that are just perfect for us.

What if we could turn envy into a guide for showing us what we would really like to have in our life?

What if envy could provide us with the motivation to make our dreams come true?

What I do, if I desire something in my life that I've observed in others, is feel how wonderful (in every cell of my body) it would be to have that show up for me. Time and time again this approach has worked and added such richness to my life in unexpected ways. For years when travel wasn't on my agenda, I would deeply tap into the excitement I'd perceive others may experience going on their trips, just because I liked the joy it created within me. Before I knew it, travel became a part of my life in such an effortless, beautiful way. Practise and see what you can create. It's so much fun. If you enjoy surprises as much as I do, embrace this approach.

Appreciation and gratitude are wonderful antidotes for envy. The more we fill ourselves up with love for our own lives, the fewer opportunities we provide for ego and envy-style thinking to take hold. When we are full of love and appreciation, we are more likely to be connected to our own guidance, believe in ourselves and follow our own pathway and purpose. Gratitude helps us to fall in love with our own lives and stay in our own lane: focused, trusting and content.

Affirmation

*I am worthy. I am good enough.
Everything I desire is already
on its way, in perfect timing
and in a perfect way for me.*

> **My tip for your path to peace**
>
> Gratitude and appreciation for all that you have and all that you are will fill you with peace. Surrender your plans to the care of the universe and trust you are exactly where you need to be, doing exactly what you need to be doing.

The essence

Envy is a great teacher if we are willing to perceive the wisdom and lessons contained within it. It shows us what we value and desire in our lives. Envy can provide us with the motivation to get free of resistance and to reach for our own stars, the dreams we haven't yet fulfilled.

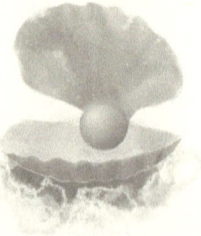

family

THROUGH FAMILY WE CAN
FLOURISH OR FLOUNDER ...
IT'S OUR CHOICE.

Our family members are our greatest teachers and our greatest supporters. They can also be critics who challenge us to rely on our own self-worth and intuition. They encourage us to grow into ourselves and to make our own decisions, gradually releasing the need for parental or sibling validation. Our family members can be mirrors for those unacknowledged aspects of ourselves. Family has a way of shining light on strengths we've been unwilling or unable to see. Family can push our buttons so that we look within at our attitudes, points of view and actions.

Family events can take us back to outdated, defined roles that we feel we either have (or should have) let go of. We can still feel limited and constrained by the expectations of our family members to carry on with these roles. This is where open communication is called for to establish new boundaries and to release expectations.

Sometimes we make the mistake of thinking that our family members should be just like us but often the opposite is true. Give your family members the gift of acceptance, allowing them to be exactly who they are. Without expectations there is less chance of hurt, and peace and goodwill can reign in your family. As energy flows where attention goes, focus consistently on the qualities you would like to see individual family members demonstrate and expect miracles.

If all else fails and you find it too challenging to be around certain family members, take care of yourself and give yourself permission to create some distance, where you limit time spent together. Sometimes space creates more peace, more gratitude and a chance to heal.

A great way to access more of our own wisdom is by observing our parents. We chose these beings as our first teachers in life. When working with clients I always remind them that our parents have always done the best they can with the inner wisdom, attributes and level of awareness that they possess. Life and our parent's lineage have shaped them and predisposed them to certain beliefs, emotional patterns and ways of functioning that we may deem to be wonderful, or not so much. From the beginning of our lives we have modelled off our parent's behaviours, often unwittingly duplicating many beliefs, attitudes and behaviours. The key is to look at our parents and make an honest and aware assessment of how they operate in order to enhance our own wisdom and knowledge of self. We have choice over what we would like to both emulate and release. We can ask, what is it about both parents that we truly admire or aspire to emulate? At the same time, we need to identify the qualities existing within our parents that it is in our best interests not to duplicate or to foster in any way. We need to reflect on those parental attributes that will be detrimental to our wellbeing, to our peace and to the reaching of our greatest potential. These are the limiting qualities that we would not desire to pass onto our children. We can change family lineages if we are willing to make conscious assessments of how we are functioning in relationship to 'inherited' family patterns. This honest approach to family legacies allows us to step up, to forgive and to avoid blame as we take responsibility for our own choices, attitudes and behaviours. With this approach we can release limiting points of view and belief systems and at the same time incorporate wonderful family values and approaches to enhance our own ways of being and seeing.

Affirmation

I am a valuable and respected member of my family. I see them and they see me through eyes of love and forgiveness. I see their beauty. I bless family interactions with light and love.

My tip for your path to peace

Peace increases when we release judgements and expectations of family members. Be willing to wipe the slate clean and start again as though it's the first time you've met. See them with fresh eyes focusing on the positive qualities they already have. Focus also on the qualities you'd like to witness to draw these attributes forward.

The essence

The family is a very complex institution. You have a choice in any moment as to how you choose to perceive and respond to family members. Release expectations and judgements to create relationships anew.

Fantasy

MAKE FANTASY A REALITY AND BREATHE NEW LIFE INTO YOUR LIVING.

Fantasy helps us to unlock our mystical magical personas. Remember that aspect of yourself that may have been Sleeping Beauty (asleep!) since childhood. Your inner child is calling you to bring elements of fantasy back to life and to enjoy the associated joy and inspiration. Fantasy helps us to remember times when wonder, awe, excitement and adventure were part of our everyday lives. Step back in time to remember what elements of fantasy resonate with you and start from there.

I asked my gifted Grade 5 literacy students what appealed to them about fantasy and how they could use it to add joy and magic to whatever they do in life. They love that in fantasy anything can happen. There are no rules; there are great challenges to solve; light always wins over dark; and lots of creative, magical solutions show up. The students felt that fantasy makes us stretch what we perceive we can become and encourages us to believe in miracles. The energy of fantasy also appealed to them with its accompanying 'dream-like, being connected to something bigger and wondrous' way. It reminded them that even objects can have an energy, a certain magic about them. Fantasy made them feel more alive. The unstoppable characters made them believe in greater possibilities.

In short, fantasy made them see life differently. It encouraged them to question and ponder what was happening in their own current realities. Themes that appealed to the group involved dragons, unicorns, magic powers, witches, wizards, and princes and princesses overcoming obstacles to be together.

Set aside time to immerse yourself in some old childhood fantasy stories and some modern-day gems like Harry Potter, to bring the energy of fantasy into your world.

Affirmation

I seek and embrace fantasy. I allow its wonders to light me up and inspire me to see the magical elements of life.

My tip for your path to peace

Balance adult 'responsibilities' with a child-like sense of wonder to bring greater harmony and peace into your world.

The essence

Indulging in fantasy can bring magic vibes, unbridled joy and a sense of wonder and possibility into any day.

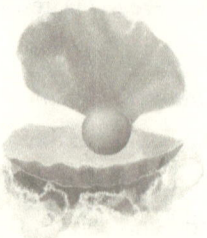

fear

BRICK WALLS WE CAN PUT UP TO LIMIT OUR POTENTIAL.

Brave people acknowledge fear, seeing it as a source of identifying what they need to heal. They often shine bright and continue regardless. Fear requires our self-compassion, as on some days its energy is more powerful than others. On 'extreme' fear days we need to be gentle with ourselves and sometimes take the less fearful option until we are in a better place to deal with the message or healing required under the fear. Fear as a word often invokes negative feelings and more fear. Work to see fear in a more positive light. Reduce the limiting power of fear by seeing it as part of an amazing guidance system for showing us what we need to overcome.

Fear can be our friend as it keeps us alert and aware on its good day. However, fear needs to be quietly in the background, not getting to make decisions that limit our choices or creative potential. If fear is left unchecked, it can gain unnecessary momentum and power, leading to more things to fear. We cannot allow fear to negatively impact our destiny by keeping us small and stuck. Fear encourages us to avoid risks to remove the possibility of disappointment or hurt. Risk-taking is where we often spread our wings, grow and change; the ego does not like that possibility. Each time we navigate our way beyond a fear, no matter how small, we take a step closer to living a life free of self-imposed limitations. Even conquering a negative emotion (fear in disguise) is a move in the direction of reaching our true potential.

Fear that runs rampant stops us in our tracks. It turns us away from everything we truly desire and keeps us 'safe and comfortable' in a little uninspired, non-expansive box. On some level fear can make us feel safe as it can be a familiar feeling. Unfortunately, fear provides a way for the ego to convince us not to hope for too much or risk failure or hurt. Fear needs to be confronted. We need to look within and face what the fear is allowing us to look away from or avoid. Being 'clear from fear' limits the chance of allowing ourselves to be held back. We can move towards discovering our treasures within and towards loving and respecting ourselves. This launches our desire to find our true path and move forward with our life's purpose.

Most of us are afraid of our own greatness. If we were willing to discover how truly amazing we were, we might have to do a few things differently. We may have to be seen and heard. We may wish to contribute and make a difference on the planet. Freedom from fear allows us to enjoy a truly creative, magical and generative life. On the other side of fear is wonder, opportunity, infinite possibilities, expansion and peace.

In the face of fear, we need to reconnect to our higher power, to regain our faith and to remind ourselves that we are safe, and all is well. If we are listening to and dwelling on fearful thoughts, we are tuned in to the voice of the ego. Messages from our higher self and guides are always positive in nature. We need to remember that we aren't given anything in life we can't handle.

When fear strikes, breathe deeply and delve into your self-care toolkit. It might be energy healing work, meditation, yoga, exercise, tapping (emotional freedom technique) or forms of creativity. Try to identify any feelings underneath the fear, and work to release them before they create a loss of momentum and dis-ease. Debilitating fear may require medical assistance and therapy.

Affirmation

I make choices that are aligned with my divine purpose. I live my life through love and joy.

> **My tip for your path to peace**
>
> Sit with the fear, initially accepting it, in order to process it from a more peaceful space. Next, identify the feelings, thoughts and emotions underneath the fear. Work to release the fear in the way that works best for you. Reiki, kinesiology, affirmations to rephrase the fear, meditation and journaling are my go-to approaches. Connect with your divine source and breathe back to peace. Remember only love is real.

The essence

Befriend your fear rather than fuelling it with increased emotion and negative thinking. Use it to get to know yourself. Allow it to assist you to become more aware of what you need to get free of, so as not to be held back. Develop strategies to give fear less intensity and to shift it with greater ease. Focus on your courage and inner light, rather than your fear. Bringing awareness to our fearful responses means that next time they can have less impact.

Food

BEAUTIFUL FUEL FOR OUR MINDS AND BODIES.

Food is for both nourishment and pleasure. Listen to your body; it often knows what it needs to consume to both heal and feel great. What it requires can vary from week to week depending on what is happening in your life. Research muscle testing as a way of determining what your body may and may not like to ingest. Sometimes we need grounding foods—think meat and potatoes—and at other times we need lighter, plant-based meals, or we might require hydrating foods. Bless your food to bring a higher, more beneficial vibration to it. Read those packages and avoid those additives. Eat organic and local produce where possible. Try to add variety to your diet to ensure the full range of vitamins and minerals are available to your body. Each fruit, vegetable or herb has a unique set of healing properties. Educate yourself so that food can be your medicine. Chew your food slowly to aid digestion, savouring each bite. Stop eating when you feel satisfied without over-filling your stomach. Avoid judging you if you over-indulge with things you know don't work for your body. Commit to making better choices next time and develop awareness around what you may be avoiding or distracting yourself from with food.

Affirmation

*I have a healthy relationship with food.
Each meal nourishes me and my body.*

My tip for your path to peace

Learn everything you can about healthy eating so that you are at peace with the choices you make around food.

The essence

There is a plethora of wonderful information out there regarding all aspects of food as medicine. Work out what eating habits help you and your body to thrive.

forging your path

TRUST YOURSELF AND ALLOW OPPOSING VIEWPOINTS TO BE WHITE NOISE.

Allow the opinions of others to stay gently in the background without deterring you from your dreams, inner guidance, pathway and course of action. Give up the need to justify your motives and actions, as often your reasoning can't be heard. Many people find it challenging to receive information that does not support or match their own reality.

Those we are connected to often mean well and are often motivated by wanting to keep us safe, limited or in a 'place' that they are comfortable with and can also relate too. When we change or up level in any way it can be intimidating for others as they can feel like they must do the same. If they are not ready for change and growth, you become threatening to the existence of the reality they are currently holding onto. If you are reading this then you are more than likely a person who desires the creation of your unique, expansive life.

It can be extremely challenging to follow our intuition and go in a direction that is not supported by those we value. Sometimes we can be questioned, criticised and made to feel 'less than'. This can then trigger feelings of self-doubt and contribute to a loss of momentum in life and trust in our choices. The strong opinions of others can undermine the fabric of who we are, but only if we allow it to. It is best to keep dreams and plans close to our hearts and avoid sharing them until they come to fruition. In this way our energy is aligned with our choices and actions without interference.

Be aware, forgive and have compassion for those who do not understand your journey. They are not meant to grasp our reality, as our path is uniquely unfolding just for us. Often we ourselves don't fully comprehend where universe is leading us. We do know, however, what feels light and right, and if we listen to our inner guidance there are no mistakes, just more and more opportunities for learning, growth and new possibilities.

I am a recovering people pleaser and conflict resolver. The problem with trying to please others (can we truly ever?) and in attempting to resolve the conflicts of others is that our energy and awareness is channelled away from ourselves. Our path is 'suspended', if only temporarily, while we attend to the needs of others. Our well-meaning connections are not privy to the big picture that we perceive unfolding.

Rise above the opinions of others. Avoid the small box of limited possibilities that comes with people-pleasing. If we repeatedly follow the advice of others, we get to live their lives. Trust yourself and your guidance from moment to moment to forge a reality that is as uniquely individual as you are. Watch and see how well-meaning people create the same reality and life repeatedly, year after year, as the thinking connected with what they perceive rarely changes. Give yourself permission to be free. Continually practise trusting yourself and your guidance system and let others enjoy their own.

An expansive life (and one that may not yet exist in this reality) is yours if you follow your heart and intuition. Those you love and whose opinions you've had to overcome will have their viewpoints challenged when you steer your own ship. From here, you may inspire others to consider new possibilities and stimulate change.

Affirmation

I give myself permission to be free of other people's opinions about me. I am not defined by the opinions of others. I trust the unique guidance that is just for me.

My tip for your path to peace

Give up people-pleasing (and adjusting yourself accordingly), as there is no peace in going against your inner knowing or resisting what is meant for you. When someone has derailed you with their well-meaning guidance, surrender the impact to the heavens to handle. Let go and let God send love and forgiveness to the 'opinionator' so you can be free of any energetic residue.

The essence

Be free of the limiting viewpoints of others. Stand still and perceive your own power and guidance. Avoid giving your power away to others by aligning with what you know isn't right for you. Trust you and the path that is uniquely unfolding for you.

Forgiveness

FORGIVE OTHERS AND FREE YOURSELF.

Forgiveness seriously tests our mettle. It's a good indication of how much we oversee our emotional reactions and thought patterns, versus the control our ego exerts. If we find ourselves wanting to be right in every situation or desiring to seek revenge in some way, then the ego is the winner. Being able to forgive releases us from the hold the other person has over our emotional life. It breaks the energetic bond that keeps the story and feelings playing on repeat between us and another. It allows healing to take place as we are willing to let go and allow some light and love to shine on the situation. There is always a lesson involved in any experience. Embracing forgiveness allows us to receive the lesson. Forgiveness encourages our willingness to return to a state of love.

Forgiveness does not condone the behaviour or require us to invite those who have hurt us back into our lives. It helps to free us from the pain that exists as a result of it. Release yourself from the burden of the pain of resentment before it impacts your health and wellbeing. Emotions and thought patterns of a negative nature impact every cell in our bodies. Unprocessed emotions create disease and disrupt the healing capacity of the body. Stress in the form of unhealthy relationships is detrimental to our health.

We all desire and require great connections. Clean up unfinished business with people so you don't have to come back next lifetime and face the same issues again with them. Consider what may be within you that may have drawn this person and situation into your life. Ask yourself, 'What am I really trying to change or release in order to grow and move forward?' Remember our interactions with others are learning opportunities. Our responses to others teach us so much about ourselves, much of which would not be possible if we existed alone. We need our relationships as they mirror back to us our strengths and weaknesses. Perceive conflict as a challenge, a way to step up, to change patterns of behaviour and to base our relationships on love and joy rather than competition. See yourself in others. We aren't as separate from others as it would seem. Forgive in others what you often can't forgive in yourself and you will get free too.

In letting things go we create the space for all of life to flow with greater ease, often in surprising new directions, as we get out of our own way. Every person is on the planet to heal and grow, even if they haven't acknowledged it yet. Allow others and yourself the opportunity to learn from indiscretions. Bring compassion to your connections with others. From here, magic, miracles and beautiful relationships can be yours.

Affirmation

I choose to see the beauty and light in each person I meet. I trust that every person is doing the best they can with the attributes they have and through the conditions in which they live.

My tip for your path to peace

Heal your relationships to bring peace to your life. Inner contentment is possible when our emotions aren't in turmoil over perceived wrongdoings of others.

The essence

The ability to forgive is an indication of a high-functioning being who is not in the grip of the ego. Forgiveness means freedom from stories and relationships that limit your potential for growth.

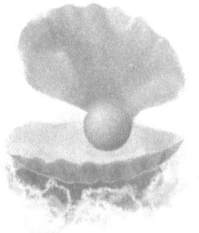

Freedom

FREE OF KARMA AND OUR
OWN LIMITATIONS ...
FREE TO CO-CREATE.

It is time to reconnect with our freedom. We've always had it, but many of us have forgotten it. Freedom is knowing in our hearts that we are always guided and safe. We trust in the universe and the divine plan as it unfolds. Freedom is about being able to express ourselves truthfully. It is being our authentic selves and making choices that are aligned with our true selves, our higher selves. It is being free of our own self-imposed limitations. It is freedom from the directives and control of the ego. It is learning our lessons effectively and being free of karma. Freedom is true abundance: the time and space to do what we love, with whom and when we choose.

To break free of the ego and experience true freedom, we need to practise observing the myriad of ways in which unease arises within us through judgement, resistance to 'what is' and avoidance of the present moment. To attain freedom, we need to move into a place of non-resistance to what is occurring for us. Acceptance and acknowledgement of our current reality allows us to be present.

Our honesty and awareness will assist us to shine the light of our consciousness on these areas, creating more freedom and peace.

> 'There is a place within you where there is perfect peace.'
> HELEN SCHUCMAN, *A Course in Miracles*

Ask yourself: Am I at ease at this moment? What's going on inside me at this moment? If you get the inner space sorted, the outside will fall into place.

Freedom can to some extent be determined by our points of view surrounding it. Freedom for me is a state of mind where I believe I am empowered and that I live in a free-will universe where all choices are possible. I can then look at what choices and changes are possible for me to move forward into greater freedom.

When we have learned from the past, released any karmic patterns and made amends as needed, we no longer require the same repetition of lessons. From here we are free of the past. We can stay present and open to new possibilities that enhance our freedom. We move into a place of truly co-creating our lives as we aren't repeating patterns based on our past limitations.

Freedom is having an abundance of opportunity and infinite potential to be explored. It is soaring above the mundane and co-creating new life regularly. Each day, month and year provides the space and opportunity to begin a new chapter.

Freedom is acknowledging our worth and trusting ourselves enough to speak our truth, be our authentic selves, set healthy boundaries and ask for our needs to be met. We allow ourselves to receive all that life has to offer and take the time to choose and follow what lights us up.

Freedom is knowing we can go where we need to go, be where we need to be and who we need to be. How do we get to true freedom? Freedom exists on the other side of our limitations. Look within and seek help as needed to get free of anything or anyone that holds you back. We need to let go of that which no longer serves us in order to make the space for that which needs to come. Freedom from guilt, freedom from self-doubt and freedom from anything that slows our ability to step into being the best version of ourselves, needs to go, to create maximum freedom. Our spirit knows the pathway; we need to listen to our inner guidance and take action to free ourselves from our limitations. We are guided through this process (even if we are unaware of it) and can release what needs to go, as we are ready.

Perceiving ourselves as spiritual beings having an earthly experience generates a greater space of freedom within us, as we don't feel that we must figure it all out and sort it all out on our own. We can receive guidance and co-create the abundant free life that the universe wants for us.

Gratitude is a wonderful way to create a space and sense of freedom, as we are focused on the wonderful things that are in front of us, rather than perceived lack. If we can make our minds feel free and limitless with lots of gratitude and positive thinking, then we are free.

Affirmation

I release all perceived limitations and restrictions to experiencing freedom of choice and the freedom to show up as myself. I look within to know myself and embrace the empowerment and freedom that comes with self-awareness.

My tip for your path to peace

Peace comes from gaining freedom from self-imposed limitations. Do the work and truly know what you need to release to be the best version of yourself. Peace arises as we make choices for our highest good and value who we are and what we are choosing.

The essence

Freedom is a high-functioning way of being. It allows us to connect with the infinite possibilities and abundance of the universe. It is the reward for looking within, releasing limiting shadow aspects and stepping into our greatness. When we are free, we know we are unstoppable.

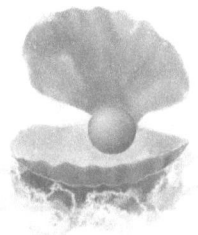

friendship

OUR FRIENDSHIPS ARE AS UNIQUE,
BEAUTIFUL AND COMPLEX AS
SHELLS ON THE SAND.

Our friendships (like all relationships) evolve as we evolve—hopefully. Some friendships become even more expansive, uplifting and enlightening over time. Other friendships dissolve as someone (or both) in the relationship changes to a point that someone or both individuals no longer feel as connected—there may no longer be the same degree of resonance. Throughout life I have experienced a full range of friendships. I am grateful for them all. Each friendship has brought joy and lessons and has helped me to be who I am today. My friendships have assisted me to know who I am, where I'm going and what I both cherish and choose to relinquish.

Some friendships nurture, support, inspire, bring joy, challenge and comfort us, add fun and laughter to our days and light us up—and some do not. The key with friendships is to have awareness: that is, knowing deeply which ones are wonderfully positive, and, at the same time, identifying those that hurt and limit. Some friendships have an expiry date—we have our wonderful connection, we receive our lessons and we part amicably. In an ideal world (one that we all contribute to with our choices) we forgive the past, we believe that all is well, and we trust that everything happens for our highest good.

Over the years, many clients have devoted sessions to understanding the complex and often tumultuous nature of their friendships. Clients have experienced a wide range of emotions and scenarios connected with their friendships. Many friendships have been laden with energy and issues needing to be cleared. Forgiveness and understanding dramatically improved the wellbeing of many clients, and they gained greater awareness of themselves, their needs and how they function in relationships of various kinds. Some friendships are beautiful connections, and others not so much. The key is to know the difference.

Much wisdom and knowledge of self is gained through challenging and even hurtful connections. From these we learn to protect our boundaries and worth, use our voice and practise the art of letting go and forgiving. The key is to know whether to hold on tightly or let go. Time is precious and so are we. We need to give ourselves permission to let go of connections that don't make us feel great, or supported or cared for.

> 'Anything or anyone that does not bring you alive, is too small for you.'
> DAVID WHYTE, POET

There is no need to burn bridges. Just realise that sometimes people aren't for you and you aren't for them. Avoid holding on too tightly.

Trust that for some connections, time may be up. You've got the lessons, you've had your day, and now they aren't going where you're going, and you're not going where they are going. Let them go their way and you go yours. Some friends come for a season, not a lifetime. Be grateful for the lessons, fun and memories that you shared. Sometimes we connect again with old friends and the connection can be even stronger, as we have healed individually and our friendship is created anew, from a greater place.

Tap into your awareness and observe 'signs' and heed your inner guidance when navigating friendships. A sign that things are changing within friendships is when things don't feel quite right in your body, when you are around certain individuals. Something may be said that seems okay, but it doesn't feel quite right to you.

Be wary of friendships that involve jealousy. There is only a small space for jealous friends. Jealous friends won't light you up and they will (often unconsciously) work to undermine you, so that they can feel better in your presence. These friends will attempt to make us feel 'less than'—once again, often unconsciously, so that their egos can convince them that they are better than us as there is something in us that is so great, that it's intimidating. These types of friends may also find reasons to judge you—to separate from you. Even worse, jealous friends can 'encourage' us to play small—to be smaller than we are—to make friends feel better, to preserve the 'friendship'.

Your aliveness, your greatness, the inspired you is the force needed in your life right now and always. Set your own light free by being the authentic, expansive you when in the company of all friends. Observe yourself and how you 'are' around the people in your life. If you find yourself aligning with gossip, complaining or becoming embroiled in some of the brands of drama and nonsense unique to some individuals, step up from this place, redirect conversation or find an excuse to quietly leave a room. Honour yourself.

There will always be those that want to put out the light in others. Make the choice to shine even brighter. If your angel wings are too much for some, spread them anyway. They are needed more than ever today.

> 'When you set your own light free
> you become a veritable force of nature.'
> DANIELLE LAPORTE

Create the space for allowing your new people, your new tribe, to step into your life by letting go of those connections that hurt and don't light you up. You are worth it, and your life and wellbeing will thank you for it. There's no need to keep fixing things that don't want or need to be fixed. Those that see you, support you, nurture you and love the person you are becoming are where your heart and energy belong. Be the kind of friend you would like to have; we draw friends to us that are like us, or who have lessons to teach us. On the other side of karmic friendships (once they are resolved and we have the lessons and forgiveness) are our true friendships.

Affirmation

I draw beautiful friendships into my life that nurture me, support me and light me up.

My tip for your path to peace

Forgive and release friendships that no longer serve you (and your highest good) to allow greater peace to flow through your life. Surrender and trust that new space is now available for beautiful connections, peaceful connections, to flow in.

The essence

We learn so much about ourselves: what lights us up, and equally what limits us, through the lens of our friendships. When looking back on our friendships (and all that they reflect) we can see who we've been, the wisdom we've acquired and where we are choosing to go. Through all the trials and tribulations, we know the energy of the beautiful souls that we desire to both continue our journey with, or call in. These are the friends we are choosing to accompany us on the next steps of our journey. What a gift they are to us; cherish them.

fun

WE ARE HERE FOR A FUN TIME,
NOT A LONG TIME.
ENJOY A BEAUTIFUL RIDE.

Each person's definition of fun should be their own, without judgement. My definition of fun has changed as I've evolved. It's less about the artificial highs that are short-lived, and more about building fun into as many moments of the day as possible. These days, it's not so much the going out and partying (although I do like to dust off my dancing shoes with friends every now and then), but more of what makes me feel warm and fuzzy, light, content or excited. Anything that makes me laugh is fun, and I can find amusement in the simplest of things. Life is my playground. I'm always looking for more opportunities for joy.

Fun is different for everyone. If you need help reaching for yours, feel free to borrow some of my suggestions:
- Hanging out with my Westies and watching their antics and personalities at play is fun.
- Swinging and chatting on our garden seat, soaking up some sun and my husband is fun.
- When my book found a publisher, I felt the crazy fun!

- Seeing my book available for purchase on Booktopia and in bookstores is great, great fun!
- Collaborating on designing the cover for this book was such a pleasure.
- Creating something new is heavenly fun. Being inspired is fun!
- Every time one of my children or my husband experiences something wonderful then my fun meter is on overdrive, as I love vicarious fun!
- The anticipation of watching a sunset as the day closes out is fun for me—especially in Santorini.
- Eating at a new restaurant excites me.
- Creating beautiful spaces and arranging flowers in my home is fun.
- Finding new pieces for my wardrobe and creating new looks is fun.
- I am super-excited sitting in my local airport because I'm eagerly awaiting a new adventure.
- Connection, conversation and laughter at family dinners are high on my fun list, as due to familiarity we are all very spontaneous and unpredictable with our conversations.
- Great inspiring conversations make me feel good.
- I find fun in being in nature and watching birds and animals do what they do.
- Reading and writing are both passion and fun.
- Learning something new is always fun for me.

Much of my fun often comes under the banner of self-care: facials, massage, acupuncture, Bodybalance, swimming, walks in nature, doing oracle card readings, meditation, decadent baths, beach and ocean time, stand-up paddle-boarding and energy healing work.

I have so much fun in my reiki business. I find my intuitive and psychic gifts super exciting as each day is totally different. The magic that arises and the changes in clients makes my work an adventure every day.

Any form of miracle or synchronicity is fun as I'm just mesmerised by how serendipitous moments come together and unfold. I find surprises to be miraculous fun. How much fun it is when something is planned for us (like my upcoming birthday trip) and we have no idea what will be happening and where we are going.

Fun is being ourself, our true self, and not holding back. We can create fun around us at any moment when we drop our guard and just be all that we are. We never know what hilarious thing might come out of our mouths at any moment. We give others permission to drop their guard and embrace fun too. When fun is a priority, we are led to more and more fun.

Many people see fun as a future thing: when I've finished this assignment/task, when I'm on holidays, when the children leave home or when I leave work or retire, I'll have fun. Fun needs to be an ingredient of the present moment. Build fun into every day. It's the most important and healing work you can ever do.

I have an adorable friend who I cherish, and so does everyone who encounters her. The thing is, this girl knows how to have fun. In fact, she's the rock star of this particular genre. She will befriend anyone who likes to have fun, with no judgement; a willingness to have fun is the only criterion. She draws people like a moth to a flame. If she moved to an isolated community 'the people' would find her.

Many might say she's 'too much' of many of the things in life we are not supposed to be, do or enjoy. The interesting thing is from this space of being herself and following her fun, I've noticed that the universe always has her back. There have been tough times, but out of nowhere the right people and situations just show up almost out of thin air. I find it hilarious that she's always so surprised by this, seemingly innocent. The energy of childlike joy and wonder has proved to be a miraculous saviour in her life. She is the perfect example of what is possible when we exist on the joy frequency and forget about the seriousness of life. Being herself has consistently given others permission to take a few risks, live life more boldly and to break free of the 'enforced confinement' of themselves. Taking to an empty dance floor and doing her version of the worm, she stunned many (out of their boredom) and created an invitation for others to hit the dance floor.

If you are having fun, then you are living the definition of a successful, high vibration life. You more than likely attract fun with ease, as like attracts like. Feelings create energy. Choose positive thinking to create both elevated emotions and high vibrational energy. People will be drawn to you and your vibe. Be prepared to be popular.

Affirmation

I am fun.
I attract the perfect version of fun for me,
each and every day.

My tip for your path to peace

Make fun a priority in all areas of life. Fun blows stress out of the water. Without stress there is calm.

The essence

Fun creates instant access to a high vibrational state. Fun feels good and our spirit and every cell in our body benefits. Fun draws all that is loving and positive to our side, such is the law of attraction.

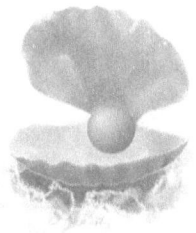

Go within

THE PLACE WHERE WE FIND
THE KEYS TO OUR KINGDOM,
COMPLETE WITH UNEXPECTED
TREASURES.

Going within is the only way to free ourselves of aspects of ourselves that don't allow us to be and receive everything we can truly be. What arises in our external world directly correlates with (and is a reflection of) our inner landscape. The handbrakes in our inner world could be the stories we tell ourselves (that become our belief systems), the old hurts that fester and grow, the limiting points of view, judgement, self-doubt or fear.

We must truly know ourselves to ascertain what we need to shift in order to heal, change and move forward. Confronting that 'within' (that we really don't want to look at) is the most challenging and liberating work we can do. It is the only way to be everything we came here to be. Often, we use distractions like shopping, gossiping, judging others, smoking, alcohol, social media or being excessively 'busy' to avoid looking at what's going on within. These distractions expertly take us away from focusing on our own issues.

Anything that we have been carrying around, that is stopping us from accessing our true potential, needs to go. It is very difficult to create the lives we desire if we are limited by or held back by our own stuff. Getting free of our wounds enables us to be who we truly are. It allows us to access the joy that we know is in there somewhere, just waiting for us to shift the heavy stuff on top, so it can shine through.

We need to access that calm space inside that gently asks to be heard. To do this we must quiet the mind to truly hear the voice of our higher selves, our truth. Finding that place of stillness, the present moment, that place of true power, has a different access point for all of us. Do you find it through yoga, meditation, reiki and other forms of energy healing? Do you find it sitting by an ocean or soaking up beauty in all its many forms? Do you find it through forms of creative expression like singing, painting and journaling, or through high-adrenaline sports? Oh, to count the ways … make sure you find yours.

Our inner guide wants to get to know us. It wants to cherish us and help us flow in life. Our inner knowing will help us make decisions with ease at the perfect time for us. Getting free of our stuff means more lightness, peace and a renewed sense of purpose.

Be patient with those working on change, including yourself. Allow yourself and others to be imperfectly perfect. Accessing all of oneself is not a linear process. We all need space and time to heal and shine in our own time.

Our healing work does not just heal ourselves. When we heal ourselves, we often heal those around us, helping to change deeply ingrained family patterns. When we make a contribution towards healing those around us, we positively affect the energy of the planet. Heal yourself and contribute to healing the world.

Affirmation

*I quiet my mind to hear my inner guide with ease.
I deeply trust my inner knowing.*

> ### My tip for your path to peace
>
> Peace comes to those who truly know and accept themselves. Peace arises when you have done the work to clear the wounds.

The essence

Brave people look within to get free of their limitations. From here infinite potential and possibilities are available. The outer world is purely a reflection of the inner world.

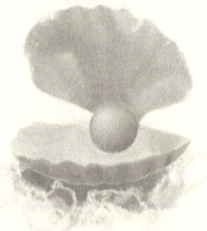

Gratitude

OPENS THE DOOR TO MAGIC AND MIRACLES.

Gratitude is a true gift to our health and wellbeing. It aligns us with the highest vibrations and power in the universe. Gratitude quietens the ego, brings a sense of peace to our lives and elevates our mood. It trains us to seek the positive and the beauty in things as our natural default mechanism. The voice in our head (that is sometimes not so friendly) doesn't get any airplay while we focus on gratitude. Gratitude allows new thinking to emerge, as we are not running the same program that the ego likes to roll with. The amazing thing about gratitude is that it has the power to raise our vibration and to bring forth even more to be grateful for. This is expansive living as we co-create with universal energy.

Gratitude brings a sense of awe and wonder to our lives. It opens the door to a childlike sense of the magic and miracles that are possible in any moment. We become seekers for magic and miracles; the more we believe, the more these occurrences reveal themselves to us.

Gratitude feels like being connected to something larger and more powerful than our human selves. For me, it is a conduit for divine energy, a source of unlimited potential and possibilities. Gratitude makes me feel powerful, as I directly impact my state of wellbeing and take pride in co-creating so much more to appreciate. As I trained myself to look for moments of gratitude, I became a greater observer of life and the synchronicities and coincidences that were moving me forward. Gratitude helps me live from a place of positive anticipation of what may occur next.

An extremely effective tool in becoming your own gratitude guru is to create a gratitude journal or simply makes notes in your daily diary, or in the notes section of your phone. Having a gratitude journal is a key factor in assisting me to focus on both small and large miracles. It helps me to stay more deeply (and for longer periods) in the space of gratitude. Be grateful for all the kindness you experience. Appreciate the seemingly small things, like lights turning green as you approach, or parking spots appearing with ease—although I do think all miracles are large ones. Complete a written or a mental gratitude list in times of joy and during times of duress. This generates positive energy and helps us cope better during challenging times. Inviting more to be grateful for to enter our lives eases suffering.

Focus on beauty to access feelings of awe and gratitude. Time in nature will provide endless opportunities for you to be captivated by beauty. Each day take a moment to focus on the beauty around you, whether in your home, at work, in your garden or wherever you walk or drive. Notice beauty in your relationships and you will experience more in your relationships to appreciate.

Affirmation

Gratitude is my natural state.
I hear words arising from others and
within that invoke feelings of gratitude.
I see all around me through
eyes of gratitude.

My tip for your path to peace

Choose daily to foster grateful thinking and watch a negative mind and associated states dissipate into the space of peace.

The essence

Gratitude has a ripple effect that flows through our lives. Focusing on what we are grateful for elevates our mood and vibration, attracting more to be grateful for. It creates the space of peace, happiness and lightness within.

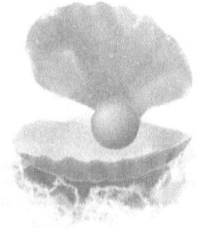

Happiness

IT'S A CHOICE.
WHAT ARE YOU CHOOSING TODAY?

One of the largest lightbulb, life-changing moments is to come to believe to one's core that happiness is found internally, not externally. No amount of attaining can equal the results of inner work. Inner work illuminates our own light, helps us to release fear, and enhances our self-worth. Taking steps to be free of limiting fear and to enhance our self-worth is vital on the journey to inner peace and happiness. Inner peace is the foundation upon which happiness can flourish.

Following what lights you up will lead you to what makes you feel happy, inspired and creative. Being creative makes us feel more alive and raises our vibration as we are focused more intently in the now. Inspiration and creativity bring joy, encourage gratitude and tune us into our connection with divine source. When we are contributing to the world in a way that feels aligned with our soul, happiness naturally follows. Adding to the happiness of someone else always contributes to our own happiness, even if we are unaware of it. This could be evident from listening to someone who hasn't been heard for a while or by showing how much someone is appreciated. Giving an individual positive attention and acceptance for who they are is uplifting for both.

Our thoughts and consequent emotions create our reality, so watch your thoughts as a plover guards her chicks … with great vigilance. Thoughts go out into the universe as beacons and return to us in some form. Tune into your emotions and reactions to discover what your triggers are, so that you can deflect negative thinking and associated emotions before they take over. It comes down to reprogramming your subconscious (automatic default) way of functioning from despairing thoughts to uplifting ones. As our feelings and patterns of thinking change, so too will our lives. Honestly assess where you are at with positive versus negative thinking. Commit to positive thoughts and positive affirmations to create a greater, happier life.

Be your own coach, constantly reminding yourself to choose to feel good and to be grateful for everything and anything. Gratitude raises our feel-good emotions and our vibration. Choose to be happy now and in the next moment and the next to build happiness momentum. When you are feeling happy use this space to remind yourself of how wonderful and powerful you truly are to generate even more happiness.

Happiness is vital to health. A content body and mind produces feel good emotions and hormones that impact all areas of our mental, emotional and physical health. Stress has less chance of taking over when our primary state is peace and happiness.

Sometimes we need to take practical steps to increase our feelings of peace and happiness.

Happiness Toolkit

Find what inspires you and learn something new.
Fill your space with beautiful things.
Give up comparing yourself to others.
Don't let your mind wander into worry and future stuff, stay in the moment and enjoy what you are doing today.
Practise self-care.
Declutter and create more space for you.
Change your scenery.
Trust in your own journey; it won't be like anyone else's.
Breathe deeply—sometimes it's that simple.
Dance.
Realise you're always enough; don't give in to self-doubt.
Keep fear in the back seat, not allowing it to make decisions that limit your life or trigger self-doubt.
Connect with those you enjoy being with and laugh.
Find a form of exercise that is fun for you.
Follow your joy.
Give up chronic 'busyness' for a simpler, more peaceful approach.
Forgive and let go of grudges.
Get some sun and connecting-with-nature time.
Look at ways to enhance your nutrition: give your body the best possible fuel.
Be grateful.

Limit your time on social media especially if it's become a bit of an addiction ... just saying.

Give up self-judgement and guilt.

Have a reiki session.

Have a hot drink, stargaze, watch the sunset, read a book, warm by the fire, enjoy the simple things.

Affirmation

I allow happiness to flow into my life in expected and unexpected ways from all directions.

My tip for your path to peace

Look within to face that which is taking away from your contentment and impacting your self-worth. From here strive for feelings of peace, which can then naturally evolve into happiness.

The essence

Channel your time and energy to where you find joy and worth, as from there it is easier to generate positivity and resulting happiness. Happiness is vital for optimal health and wellbeing.

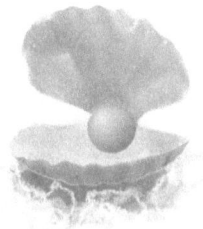

Healing journey

OPTIMAL HEALTH IS OUR DIVINE RIGHT. EMBRACE THE BELIEF THAT LIFE AND OUR BODIES ARE HEALING US EVERY HOUR OF EVERY DAY.

We are all on some kind of healing journey (whether it be physical, mental or emotional) from the moment we arrive on the planet until the moment we leave, even if we haven't acknowledged it yet. We are here to heal ourselves, others and the planet. With our intent and commitment to heal come the right material, people, information, therapists and doctors to assist our process.

Believe you are healed by focusing on your wellness more than the illness. Convince your mind it is well. For me, what shows up in my body appears to be manifested or maintained by my mind and its thought processes. By focusing on my inventory of symptoms each morning, I was inadvertently reminding my mind of them and keeping them in place. Each day I'd connect with how the illness made me feel and lock it further into my body. It was as though I was reminding my body (through my mind) to keep the dis-ease in place. How things began to change once I identified this pattern and set about to convince my mind, which in turn convinced my body, that it was well. Sometimes (to our detriment) we can become so identified with our bodies that we forget we are spiritual beings who directly influence our wellbeing with our emotional and mental responses.

Don't let a diagnosis define you. Get advice from the medical profession and also look at nutrition as medicine and other healing modalities. Be proactive and intuitive regarding your healing. It can be overwhelming with so much conflicting and contrasting information. For example, one point of view about auto-immune conditions is that the body attacks and damages its own tissues, decreasing the body's ability to fight invaders, whereas alternative viewpoints (such as in the work of Anthony William) tell us that auto-immune conditions are really our body fighting undetected viruses and pathogens and that if we deprive viruses and bacteria of their favourite foods (gluten, dairy, eggs, toxins and stress), then we give our bodies a fighting chance of healing. Anthony also reminds us that our bodies are constantly working to heal us. We need to help rather than hinder our healing process by listening to our intuition about our health, trying what works and never giving up until we have the optimal health we deserve.

Educate yourself about nutrition. Avoid processed foods laden with additives. Read those labels. Eat foods that are seasonal and as close to the source as possible. Research the specific healing properties of various fruits, vegetables, herbs and spices. Nature has provided all we need for optimal health.

Avoid crash diets as they are non-nurturing and therefore non-enduring. When we starve ourselves or overindulge, we are often trying to control a feeling we don't want to feel. This approach to eating blocks the inner guidance system. We are pushing down the feeling that wants to be felt, when it needs to be released and healed. In not allowing a feeling to emerge, we prevent healing. We have to feel the feeling to heal and be free. If you've over-indulged, let go of guilt, as there is no place for guilt in a life of celebration, joy and peace. Instead recommit to healthy habits that nurture body, mind and spirit.

Whatever your current health reality is, accept what is, stay positive and get to work on getting free of dis-ease. The power of prayer and positivity has brought miraculous results to many. The mind is a very powerful tool and we need to fill it with positivity and faith that will assist our healing. Laughter is medicine. It shifts stress and creates joyful healing states.

Exercise and therapies designed to ease stress and promote wellbeing are great contributors to healing. Nurture, nurture, nurture yourself, and dress and behave like a well person, as you are climbing back to wellness.

To move forward always recognise the growth that's already taken place within you and celebrate any new awareness you are adding to your life.

What are you here to change, heal or achieve? What else can get even better in your life? We all have great intentions, yet sometimes we can be a little thrown off course.

Push yourself to get free of things that limit you. Don't resist, let go of what needs to go and be willing to 'see'. Get free of old baggage and embrace renewed clarity, strength and recognition of your desires and where you want to be for the next chapter of your life. It can be tumultuous as you unearth things that are calling out to be healed on all levels.

Healing the past (and being free of wherever its effects may have landed in your mind, heart, body and life) is essential for new horizons to beckon. Life becomes more inspired when nothing and no-one holds us back. Just as a physical detox needs to be undertaken gently so as not to be detrimental to our health, we need to release long-standing emotional and mental patterns in a compassionate way (that is manageable for us) to optimise success. We are blessed on this planet to have amazing doctors, surgeons, therapists and healing modalities of all kinds. Be guided to what is perfect for you.

Affirmation

In this moment I claim my divine right to enjoy optimal health. I am naturally drawn to all that is available to unburden myself from anything that limits my potential for healing.

My tip for your path to peace

Do whatever is possible to maintain a high vibrational state of love, joy and worth. This invokes peace and optimises our healing potential.

The essence

Look within to discover your own unique blueprint for healing. Your spirit knows what you are holding onto that is limiting your healing and growth; equally it knows what you require to thrive. Connect and listen.

Inner child

HEAL YOUR INNER CHILD TO PROMOTE DEEP HEALING OF THE ADULT YOU.

Our childhood creates the lens through which we see, perceive and respond to situations, events and people in our adult lives. If your needs weren't met as a child there is a fair chance they may not be met now. Many adult 'tantrum-like' behaviours are old, conditioned patterns and responses to not having our needs met as children. If we haven't healed these patterns we are triggered by the same scenarios on repeat.

Talking to, comforting and reassuring our inner child (just as we would any small child) goes a long way to making us feel safe, protected and worthwhile. Our parents did the best they could with the skills they had. Now it is up to us to take over from where they left off. As you climb into bed at night, go back in time for a moment to any place or space that did not feel comfortable to you as a child. Reassure your inner child that all is now well, that there is nothing to feel guilty or ashamed of, as you were only a child and could not often influence the actions of adults around you. If you felt powerless, reassure him or her that you are now in charge of your own destiny and have everything you need to make choices for creating a great life.

Enjoy moments to remind yourself of positive childhood experiences and of times you felt free of responsibility, stress, finances, obligations and the opinions and desires of others.

Step back in time and embrace the magical energy you had as a child. Bring this vibrant energy back into your daily life. To do this, we might: stay open to magic and surprises; expect miracles even when faith is challenged; and trust in the inherent good in others and help them to see it within themselves. We could: indulge in fantasy; play, laugh and be spontaneous; embrace a sense of curiosity, awe and wonder; and remember what we loved doing as children and see if we can bring it back to life, or find the adult version. We may choose to: lighten up; do work that we love; be grateful, stay in the moment; let the past be the past and allow the future to take care of itself; and remember every day should be a celebration.

Affirmation

*I listen to, hear with ease and value
the wealth of information coming
from my inner child.
He or she transforms and heals
me so I can step into being
the best version of myself.*

> **My tip for your path to peace**
>
> Reassuring and listening to your inner child brings greater peace to now.

The essence

Spend time with your inner child to gain both insight and healing for your adult self. Nurturing, acknowledgement, compassion and understanding are key.

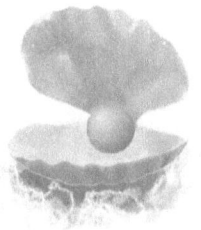

Inspiration

SURROUND YOURSELF WITH THE PEOPLE AND IDEAS THAT INSPIRE YOU, TO GAIN THE MOST FROM LIFE.

Inspiration is being mentally stimulated to the point that we do or feel something, often something creative. It can be in the form of sudden insight or a brilliant idea, or a hit of intuition, showing up just when we need it. For me, it's a state that I like to maintain continually, as it's linked intrinsically to my wellbeing, motivation and sense of purpose in life. Many feel that inspiration means 'of spirit', so if we are connected to our divine source and intuition, we live an inspired life.

There is a positivity, joy and peace that comes from living through inspiration. Our job is to seek the inner spark and that which lights us up in life, as that's the place from which much inspiration originates.

> 'When you are inspired your consciousness expands in every direction.'
> WAYNE DYER

What lights you up and inspires you?

I am inspired by great conversation with like-minded souls.

Kind words, appreciation and gratitude light me up.

I am inspired by great literature that causes me to reflect on my own way of being and promotes personal growth.

The power and beauty of crashing waves on beaches light me up.

I am inspired by flowers and their intricate, unfolding, mesmerising beauty.

My garden, my own sanctuary, lights me up and brings forth creative ideas in abundance, matching the abundance of nature.

Music encourages me to go within and to know myself more.

Beauty and pleasure in all their forms light me up.

Fashion is creative heaven for me.

The power of laughter lights me up.

Beautiful stationery and books light me up.

Travel inspires me as I see cultures in new ways and am exposed to new ideas, points of view and ways of seeing the world.

Great mentors and speakers inspire me as they challenge my thinking and reaffirm what I am processing or striving to be.

The more you know yourself and what inspires and lights you up, the more you connect with your inner wisdom and peace.

Affirmation

*I regularly quiet my mind.
I go within to access inspiration
and to discover what
lights me up.*

My tip for your path to peace

Making space to be inspired and identifying what lights us up lead to a peaceful life, as we are not resisting the flow of life, or where it wants to lead us.

The essence

Knowing ourselves and what inspires us gives us direct access to our inner wisdom and peace. Life can flow beautifully from here.

Intuition

IT'S A FORCE BEYOND COMPARE ...
ARE YOU TRULY LISTENING?

Intuition is our secret, beautiful weapon in creating a life of flow and inspiration. Intuition is a gift from the heavens, letting us know we are both connected to source energy and supported. Committing to a healing path and healing ourselves spiritually, emotionally, physically and mentally are essential in order to access the full spectrum of our intuition. The more whole and healed we are, the clearer the channels are for hearing our inner wisdom.

Our intuitive connection (and wellbeing) is negatively impacted by fearful, ego-generated thinking. If we are listening to the voice of the ego, the messages coming through from our inner guide are scrambled or incoherent. Consistently staying in the present moment and aligning with positive thoughts help us to bypass the demands of the ego and open to our innate intuition. To hear the wisdom within, connect regularly with your heart space through breathing and centering. Breathe deeply and stay present to quieten ego-based thinking; enhancing your intuitive connection. Being centered, balanced, clear and grounded in our energies helps us to access our inner wisdom. Trusting ourselves and the guidance we receive helps intuitive insights to flow even more freely and abundantly.

The path to accessing our intuitive abilities involves working to gain freedom from fear. Fear is a low vibrational state and blocks intuition. Conversely, focusing on love (a high vibrational state) in all its many forms—appreciation, respect, gratitude, kindness, nurturing and compassion—supports divine connection and access to our intuitive higher selves.

Intuition is our divine compass, always pushing us in the right direction to follow our guided paths, those we have been aware of since before we were born. Some great tools for developing our intuitive skills through quieting the ego and its associated fear-based thinking are: setting positive daily intentions; lighting a candle and focusing on your own inner light; enjoying nature and sunshine; breathing deeply; creative pursuits; gratitude for small things; eating mindfully; swimming in the ocean; and clearing clutter from our homes, workspaces and minds. Oracle cards, yoga, reiki and meditation are all great ways to quieten the mind and access the wisdom of our higher selves.

Affirmation

*I still my mind and have
full access to my intuition.
I hear my inner messages
and follow them for
my highest good.*

> **My tip for your path to peace**
>
> Taking steps to quiet ego-based thinking and stay in the present moment is essential for developing a peaceful mind that is open to the wisdom of our inner guide.

The essence

Life flows with greater ease and contentment when we access our inner wisdom and trust it when making choices and taking action for our highest good.

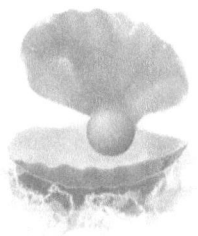

Joy

LET IT UNFOLD IN ALL ITS
UNEXPECTED AND MAGICAL WAYS.

Joy is our catalyst for change and expansion. It raises our vibration and attracts more situations, people and circumstances for creating more joy. A mission this lifetime is to find our joy. The pathway of our highest good is drawn to us through joy. Following what lights us up more readily connects us with our life purpose.

What is it that so far you've only dreamt of that you'd truly like to have show up in your reality? We need to be honest with ourselves and look at (and then banish) the excuses and justifications we have in place for not receiving the infinite possibilities available to us. We need to replace all 'what ifs' and 'buts' with belief in ourselves. Removing all self-imposed limitations will bring us closer to our joy. You are the only person in life that can stop you. Being free to follow our hearts, and experience our dreams coming true, brings joy.

Ask the universe for assistance, put questions out there. For example, 'What would it take for … to show up in my life?'

Observe, listen and excitedly anticipate how things will unfold without being vested in outcomes; maybe the universe has an even better plan. Follow your intuition and take action steps to move forwards where inspiration leads you. Trust in divine flow.

Laughter is a counterpart of joy. It raises our vibration and clears stress and unwanted emotions. It lightens our load and that of others. We feel a sense of release, relief and peace afterwards. Each time you laugh you give yourself a gift. If you can make someone else laugh you add magic and healthy emotions to their day. What can you find humour in today? There are opportunities for laughter in any moment. We can choose to see the funny or serious side of things that are presented to us in life.

Make time to care for you and nurture your self-worth. Feeling joy is initially an inside job. As you begin to feel wonderful about who you are, joy naturally arises. Joy is such a high vibrational state that it attracts abundance and miracles of all kinds.

Joy naturally arises when we are connected to our divine self, as we embrace all that life presents, knowing that even the challenges are opportunities to grow and evolve. Joy is wonderful for our planet, as when we are in a state of joy, we like others to experience this too. We care more deeply, and we like to serve. Our desire to be of service makes a positive impact on all those we encounter.

Affirmation

I allow my joy to unfold and I expect miracles in expected and unexpected moments.

> **My tip for your path to peace**
>
> Takes steps to follow what lights you up; and watch your joy and peace with what life presents begin to unfold.

The essence

To make dreams come to fruition we need to find self-belief, self-worth and joy. High vibrational states allow us to attract what we most require and desire.

Keeping confidences

THE BIRTHPLACE OF AUTHENTIC AND LOVING COMMUNICATION.

Keeping confidences is how we gain self-respect and respect from others. We rarely trust gossips, as we have a sense of unease, along with knowing that they in turn will gossip about us.

To have a high vibration life (which is one that draws constantly things that delight, surprise and inspire) we need to choose a matching way of functioning. Along this path, step one is to be impeccable with our word. This takes practice, as for many of us when we pass on things we shouldn't there's an immediate feeling of being valuable and powerful. We have a captive audience that gives the ego a little hit of validation. However, the flip side is that hours or days after breaking a confidence or passing on information that we know we shouldn't we often experience a sense of unease, a feeling that we are not good enough, often not knowing why. Women are particularly prone to this because our ego and self-worth often crave attention and validation from others.

All forms of gossip keep everyone functioning at a low vibe as it usually involves some form of drama, upset, unease, problems rather than solutions, comparison, competition and judgement. It's how the 'dark' wins, but we need to spread light. If we grow up around people who gossip, we can be unconsciously taught to function in this way as we aren't shown anything different, and we aren't aware of the negative energy that surrounds it. Before we know it gossip becomes the primary form of communication.

We can't judge ourselves for this; we just need to keep trying to overcome it through awareness and commitment. There are signals that our spirit gives us that something is not right. For me, I could always feel when something that shouldn't be repeated was brewing up wishing to 'express' itself. I would then lock the information down fast. Eventually, as the pattern is broken, it stops happening and we become like a vault: very good at storing treasure (in the form of confidences) within.

Confidentiality can enhance wellbeing. Often when people are diagnosed with an illness, they request privacy, choosing to share the ordeal with and lean on only a few trusted loved ones. Well-meaning people often spread the news like wildfire as they feel they are being sympathetic and caring. Unfortunately, this creates a vibe of focusing on a person's illness rather than their wellness, which hinders healing. The soul needs to be able to focus on wellness, not illness, to heal. People can inadvertently feed the illness machine by talking about it and dwelling on how sick the person has become

Keeping confidences allows us to step into a different way of living, connecting and communicating. Our self-worth increases as we value our integrity. Opportunities to judge ourselves are limited and our emotional wellbeing increases. People confide in us, instilling confidence. Our relationships are enhanced as they are based on mutual respect and trust. We can communicate honestly and effectively, always expressing what wants to be expressed. We know our friends have our back.

Affirmation

*I am impeccable with my word.
I value my integrity.
My communication style with others is
always positive.*

My tip for the path to peace

Peace prevails when communication is respectful, as there is no sense of unease or guilt present when confidences are honoured.

The essence

The way we communicate can define us. Strive to be impeccable with your word and maintain confidences to engender respect from others and within yourself.

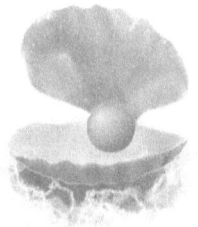

Kindness

START FIRST WITH KINDNESS TO
SELF AND ALLOW IT TO FLOW
TO OTHERS.

Kindness fills our hearts with love and warmth. It sends healing energy throughout our bodies and lives. In giving to others, we truly receive. What we put out into the universe comes back to us in some way, so kindness enhances our lives and those of others in immeasurable ways. Each day ask, 'How may I serve?' In being guided to serve, the universe also serves us: we receive in unexpected ways. Words have weight, they can hurt and uplift. What we put out comes back to us, so make it count.

Take care of your solar plexus chakra through reiki or some other form of energy healing. If our self-worth and personal power are enhanced through a balanced solar plexus chakra, we are more likely to be kind to ourselves. We will then create experiences that nurture and support us. We will have more energy for gifting to others.

What might kindness look like for you? Kindness could be a smile to a stranger or cooking a meal for loved ones. It is patting an animal that is always there to greet you when you come in the door. It is giving flowers just because, or using words that uplift another. It could be indulging in loads of self-care without guilt and being generous with your time. Filling up your own cup and only giving what is flowing over the sides is vital. If we are depleted our giving can be less effective as we may feel hidden resentment and frustration (as our own needs aren't being met) and the giving may not be as powerful.

Gratitude for the smallest things spreads kindness. People love to feel appreciated and valued. Enjoy the ripple effect that kindness creates as it reminds others of how great kindness feels and encourages them to spread more of the same. With kindness we start to change the world one person at a time.

Develop generosity of spirit, giving freely where you have an abundance of time and resources. The universe will then be generous with you, often in unexpected, surprising and miraculous ways.

Affirmation

*I look for ways to spread kindness.
I trust that I will uplift others
and in return receive blessings of
kindness in surprising ways.*

> **My tip for your path to peace**
>
> Create peaceful feelings and peace in your life by taking steps to add small acts of kindness to your daily living.

The essence

Kindness is healing medicine for ourselves and others. It is the healing energy the planet requires for peace.

Leaving the planet

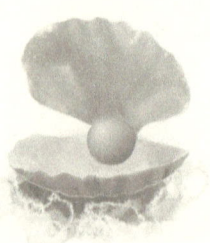

MAKE SURE THERE IS NOTHING LEFT UNSAID, UNDONE OR UNLOVED.

Leaving the planet is cause for celebration. It is a celebration of the healing journey and the mission(s) of this lifetime reaching completion. We get to have a continuation of our 'living' in a heavenly space, once our earth 'boot camp' time is complete.

We need to grieve for our loved ones in ways that are uniquely our own, in order to enhance our healing. Focusing on the love we have for them helps us to heal, and facilitates the ability of our loved ones to move on. Our loved ones can more readily connect with us and help us grow on our journeys from a space of love.

Any time spent on earth is a complete life. For example, just seeing a sunset may be the mission for some souls. We all arrive with vastly different plans for our life on earth. Length of time on earth is not a predeterminer for a successful life. We must trust that our 'exit point' is divinely guided.

Make sure you've unleashed your best 'work' every day so that you can be proud of the imprint you leave behind. Work is wherever we expend our time and energy each day: it could be raising children or running a fashion house. Listen carefully throughout your life to those intuitive urges of your spirit so you can 'die well', being content that you did everything you could to be the best version of yourself, to heal what needed to be healed, and to make the dreams meant for you become a reality.

Make sure you loved well, forgave well, judged less and made the best of the circumstances, tools, gifts, talents and abilities you were blessed with for your lifetime. Free yourself of ego-dominated thinking, as it's a much more peaceful and inspiring space to live.

Attempt to find heaven on earth by surrendering to a higher power, letting go of control, freeing yourself from fear and co-creating with divine guidance. Achieving heaven on earth before leaving the planet can be assisted through meditation, prayer, affirmations, music, connecting with nature and reading inspiring and thought-provoking literature. Consistently looking within to identify and heal our shadow aspects, valuing and seeking opportunities for personal growth, and understanding our true selves are essential aspects of dying well. Finding beauty and love everywhere and living from a place of gratitude and appreciation are ways to bring heaven closer to earth.

Affirmation

I create heaven on earth through my words, thoughts and actions.

> ### My tip for your path to peace
>
> Have no resistance to unleashing your best work every day. Being pleased with the contribution we are making to our lives and to those of others, creates peace within.

The essence

Leaving the planet is to be celebrated rather than feared. When we connect to universal guidance and co-create our lives with the divine, we will be proud of the legacy we leave behind. Grieve for loved ones when they pass and focus at the same time on the love and beautiful memories. You will meet again, and won't that be a celebration.

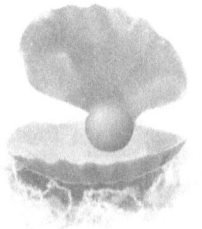

Lessons

BE A STUDENT OF LIFE.

Remaining open to learning and pursuing learning are vital for our brain health and general wellbeing. Learning is essential for effectively navigating life through all its wondrous and challenging elements.

Take your medicine (your lesson) as it arrives, without resistance. Avoid creating limiting excuses for not seeing and hearing whatever is required for your personal growth. Be a student of the 'onwards and upwards' school. Reach the top of your own class, your greatest potential, the best version of yourself.

The miraculous nature of life is that we are presented with the exact lessons, delivered in the perfect way, from the right person, just as we require them. We need to drop control, let go of the insidious urge to be right, and just receive the lessons as they are presented. Allow time for each lesson to assimilate. Rest assured that if we don't get the new lesson, truth or awareness, the universe will set up other opportunities for us to do just that. Some lessons we really don't want repeated, so it's beneficial (and a more peaceful way to live) if we can stay aware and be receptive. This stance allows our 'lessons' to pass with ease and lightness, accompanied by new perspectives and growth.

Remember, anything in life that we strongly react to or resist may have the greatest teachings and potential learning intertwined. Be open to changing yourself and your points of view as often as possible, to maximise all that you and your life can be.

Affirmation

I readily receive the lessons that are woven especially for me into the fabric of my life.

My tip for your path to peace

Avoid resistance to seeing and hearing truths and lessons as they arise. Embracing and learning our lessons, along with clearing that which no longer serves us, creates the space for more peace to surround our lives.

The essence

Be a gold-star student of life by opening your consciousness and awareness to the miraculous opportunities for growth and learning that are presented for us daily.

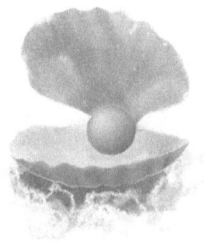

Life purpose

FOLLOW YOUR JOY TO FIND YOUR PURPOSE.

Sometimes our lives seem 'unsettled' because we want to discover that magical life purpose, the one that will set us on our path and make our life feel complete; life handled, box ticked. What if it was simpler than that? What if just following our joy, the things that light us up, is all that is required to allow life to unfold as it's meant to, drawing to us exactly what we require, from moment to moment? While in this space, we need to listen to our inner voice. When we are clear and content, the voice of the ego quietens, and we can more readily hear our inner wisdom.

Our inner voice is always present, gently nudging us in the right direction. Connecting with our life purpose is a slow reveal. It is achieved by adopting a lifetime approach of taking steady, guided, step-by-step action. We aren't generally given the whole package in a day. Listening to your intuition and taking guided action is essential in bringing forth your life purpose at a more rapid rate.

Many clues are given to us throughout life about directions in which we may love to travel. Possibilities for our life path can be found in our childhood loves, our current interests and in anything that inspires us or draws out our creativity and inspiration.

Sometimes heading in the 'wrong direction' is necessary to force us to abandon that path and forge a new one. Each new discovery leads to more expansion, direction and inspiration. Before you know it, you will be right where you need to be, making the impact you need to make ... so celebrate that today.

Affirmation

*My path ahead is clear as I am drawn naturally
to that which brings me joy.
I listen to both the whispers of the universe
and of my intuition, to move effortlessly
in the direction I am destined:
for my highest good.*

My tip for your path to peace

Listening to and responding to the whispers of our intuition promotes peace within, as we are offering no resistance to the guidance we are receiving.

The essence

Following a path that sparks joy, listening to our intuition and taking inspired action is essential in bringing forth our life purpose at a more rapid rate.

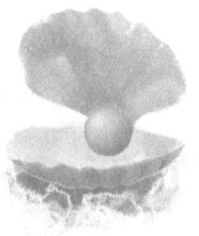

Love

IT REALLY DOES MAKE THE WORLD
GO ROUND ... AND FORWARD.

'Love is all there is.' Such a simple statement and shrouded in so much truth. Feel the energy of love as often as you can, wherever you can. The love that you feel for yourself is radiated around you. Work on unconditional love for yourself to enhance all your relationships. The love we feel for ourselves is mirrored back to us. Constantly think of those things that create love in your heart and allow it to build and flow throughout your body and into your life. Love heals dis-ease, raises our vibration and helps create a world that we'd truly like to inhabit. Remember that only love is real. All the rest is ego reaction, fear, taking things on for others and disconnection from our source. A question that I love to ask (and I always eagerly wait for responses) is, 'How can life show me it loves me?'

When embracing the energy of love try to see that all experiences and people have value. They are our teachers, showing us where we are (via our reactions) on the scale of love. Accept what is and always stay open to learning more about yourself. From the space of self-awareness, it is easier to move back to love as we have a greater understanding of our motivations and reactions.

Creating a beautiful, love-filled life truly is an inside job. Loving and approving of ourselves is the greatest gift we can give to ourselves. The world around us will catch on and shower us with more love. We need to give to ourselves the same love (kindness, compassion, nurturing, gratitude, appreciation) that we are willing to give to others. Filling up our own cup (and having it so overflowing that it spreads to all our relationships and experiences) is essential for self-love and self-care.

Ask to see all people and situations through the eyes of love, and watch miracles unfold as judgement and negative emotions slip away. A gentle peace can then be the undercurrent of our lives.

Start with watching all your thoughts like the shepherds of old watched their sheep. Make sure your thoughts are lifting you up rather than beating you down. This is a moment-to-moment choice that will make love bloom within you and flow into your life. If it is not love, it doesn't belong in your mind and your world.

Gratitude for everything and anything immediately connects us to the vibration of love. There is no space for unkindness to self and others when gratitude is flowing freely and working its miraculous magic on our hearts and lives.

Affirmation

*I love and appreciate all aspects of myself
and allow love to flow within me
and around me constantly.
I am connected to an ever-present,
powerful source of love.*

My tip for the path to peace

Surrender anything that is not bringing you peace to the universe to handle. Give up attempting to do it all on your own; it's exhausting. Trust and let go.

The essence

Love heals and transforms. It shows us the way. It leads us out of our darkness into our light. Love allows us to shine our light to best serve ourselves and others.

Magic and miracles

SOMETIMES THE DOOR CHOOSES YOU
... ARE YOU READY TO OPEN IT?

Open to the possibility of magic becoming the predominant theme of your life. To do this, constantly cherish and be grateful for the beauty that surrounds you. Love all that you are and all that you have. Notice miracles no matter how large or small, to draw more of them towards you. To receive miracles, we need to become a living miracle. We open the door to our own miraculous nature and to our ability to manifest miracles by embracing the miraculous qualities of love, compassion, honour, truth, integrity, faith, trust in our divine connection, willingness to serve, generosity of spirit, kindness, respect, gratitude and appreciation.

Become the magical state of awe and wonder that inhabits our childhood existence. Embrace magic. Take yourself back into the world of unicorns, fairies, wizards and dragons to remind you of the energy and aliveness of magic. Imagine what it would be like to be a magical being. What superpowers do you have waiting to come forth?

Every day holds the potential for new magic. Our responses to all that life presents offer opportunities for magic and miracles. Every time we get free of something that once limited us, or choose loving reactions over fearful responses, we are making miracles as we open to new possibilities in these momentous moments. You have lots of magic inside you and it's time you let some of it out to give to yourself and share with the world. What magic could you be today?

Count the small blessings and miracles as they arise to create the momentum of more miracles and magic. Great vibes draw miracles to us. Alignment with high vibrational energies of love, joy, gratitude, appreciation, peace and compassion help in the manifestation of all that we desire and require. Choose fun and all that lights you up as many times as you can during the day. Expect magic and miracles and they will appear. Our belief in miracles must outweigh our doubt or scepticism around such phenomena.

Some of my mini-miracles include: going to pay for an item and discovering I had unexpected and unexplained store credit; a client cancelling so I could leave on an exciting trip early; getting a parking spot right outside a busy hotel; a decadent room upgrade on a recent trip; my son's appointment being scheduled on the same day as mine (at the other end of the state) so we could travel together; beautiful out-of-the-blue compliments; smiles from strangers; seeing a white peacock and a white wallaby for the first time; synchronistic signs; serendipitous moments; unexpected invitations, gifts and financial windfalls; and beautiful birds appearing outside my rooms as each reiki client leaves.

My tiniest 'large' miracle came after listening to a speaker talk about the importance of just being. 'Just *be*,' was his mantra for staying in the present moment. As I was leaving the conference there was something attached to the end of my fingertip: my friend and I were flummoxed and flabbergasted (and every weird word under the sun) to discover a tiny sticker on my finger that said, 'Be'. How it got there I will never know. It reminded me that living a conscious life attracts miracles and magic of all kinds.

To attract miracles, we need to be willing to be a miracle in this world. A game changer for me has been asking:

'What miracle can I be in this world?'

'What miracles can I create today?'

Wayne Dyer says, 'Your miracles are an inside job. Go there to create the magic you seek in your life.' Do the inner work relentlessly so that nothing stands in the way of drawing miracles into your world.

Affirmation

I believe in the magic of the universe.
I am a conduit for miracles,
and they show up for me
every day.

My tip for your path to peace

Find ways to surrender, forgive and let go of that which no longer serves you, to create the fertile ground for magic to arise in your life. There is peace in trusting and expecting (rather than forcing) magic and miracles to manifest in your reality.

The essence

Be willing to ask for the extraordinary, and maintain a vibration of joy, faith and love as catalysts for bringing forth magic and miracles.

Meaning

BE A TRUE EXPLORER: LOOK WITHIN AND NAVIGATE YOUR WAY TO INNER PEACE AND PURPOSE.

Finding meaning in our lives is essential for happiness and inner peace. If we perceive purpose in our lives, we feel content knowing that we are on track: we are achieving what we came here to accomplish, even if this is on a subconscious level. Meaning and purpose allow us to lead our own lives and to be a beacon, a guide for others. Inner healing provides the foundation for finding meaning in our lives.

To live a life of meaning and purpose we need to heal a lifetime of often unacknowledged wounds, patterns and limiting attributes. We can't do that until we are willing to 'see' without the array of distractions we use to avoid the hardest work of all: looking within. The external world does not have all the answers, but we sure do. All the power for change lies within, just waiting to break through. When we confront our shadows, we undertake healing even if we are not aware of this happening. Free of the influence of our fearful ego functioning, we can move forward in life with greater ease.

What does healing mean for you?

For me, healing is a part of every moment of life. Inner knowledge is true wisdom. I am a sponge for learning about me and how I roll! Healing is being honest with myself and reflecting on my thoughts, words and actions. If I feel any sort of unease, I immediately stop, breathe deeply and look within to see what is under the emotion, to determine what is really going on.

I endeavour to catch myself giving into distractions from the outside world that I may be using to avoid addressing what is really going on for me. I look at my choices and determine whether they are moving me forward in life and enhancing my health, wellbeing and potential. From here I know I am on purpose and life is filled with meaning. I am living an inspired life.

Affirmation

I let go of all masks and pretences and honestly look within to find that which limits me living my best life. I release; I surrender all that holds me back.

My tip for your path to peace

Inner peace is the gift we create or restore within ourselves through our healing work. Life is peaceful and has greater meaning when we are healed and not resisting following our path. Inner peace is the result of knowing who we are and where we are going and at the same time being grateful for this wonderful state of being.

The essence

Our healing work leads us to find our own inner sanctuary. It is a place free of self-imposed limitations from where we seek meaning and purpose. We engage in the flow of life without needing to control everything. We trust ourselves to make great choices that move us forward.

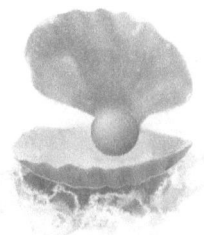

Meditation

EVOLVE INTO YOUR HIGHER SELF
... AND TAP INTO YOUR UNLIMITED POTENTIAL.

We are spiritual beings having a human experience. Meditation helps us to reconnect to our spiritual source. It helps to free us from the chains of conditioned patterns and programs as it forges new neural pathways and a 'new' us that isn't conditioned by the past.

Most of us have a term for the universal intelligence and presence that guides us. Meditation is key for anyone interested in connecting with the universe, source, God, or the divine, in a way unique for them. Through meditation, we get to be our divine self (in our human body), co-creating our lives with greater ease and flow. Through meditation we access our abilities, gifts and full potential. Our lives become more meaningful and purposeful.

Meditation is for you what stills your mind and helps you connect to your heart, your inner voice and universal wisdom. Meditation can be simply what occurs when you get into the present moment or your zone of contentment. This can be experienced with any kind of sustained focus such as playing sport or pursuing creative interests. A meditative state can be achieved through anything that takes you out of your head, to be fully present in the moment. In this space we are receptive to receiving messages from our higher self, as the voice of the ego is quietened or non-existent.

Meditation doesn't have to be a formalised practice such as listening to recordings or guided by an instructor. However, these approaches promote deep healing, peace and spiritual growth, as they have often been developed by experts in the field and great spiritual teachers. Guided meditation is great when we are first delving into this area, assisting us to more quickly discover and access a new way of being.

In any space of stillness that we create, we open our potential for healing and to hearing the guidance we've been asking for. We receive flashes of brilliance and inspiration that are within us and waiting to be unlocked.

Meditation has benefits for all aspects of our physical and emotional wellbeing. When our bodies and minds are balanced, stress is reduced, and our bodies have greater strength to carry out the tasks they so beautifully perform.

Meditation allows us to access our source, our wisdom and our power, and as such provides the greatest way for us to be free of our habitual limiting patterns. Free of our past conditioning we have the potential to create a new destiny, one that is more aligned with who we are desiring to become.

Affirmation

*I choose to quieten my mind
so that I can hear the universal wisdom
that is always available to guide me,
free me, inspire me and heal me.*

My tip for your path to peace

Making meditation a part of our daily life will bring a peaceful calm and clarity to all our undertakings. Those around us will benefit from our peaceful glow, presence and wisdom.

The essence

Meditation helps to connect us to the spiritual world and to co-create our lives with divine assistance and greater freedom from any earthly limitations. We attune to a higher frequency, raise our vibration and manifest our desires with greater ease.

Mindfulness

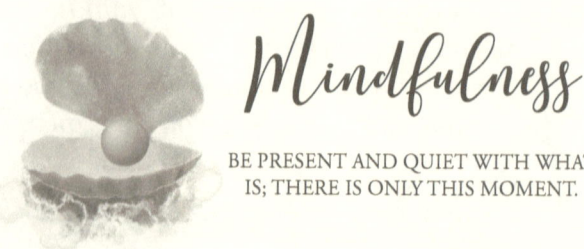

BE PRESENT AND QUIET WITH WHAT IS; THERE IS ONLY THIS MOMENT.

Mindfulness implies a way of being and living that maximises staying in the moment, being open and aware, and creating peace through quieting experiences. It's about accepting what is, without judgement.

Mindfulness has a beneficial impact on our health and wellbeing as it trains our minds to be present, focused and positive. If or when stressful situations do arise, we are in a better place to effectively handle what needs to be handled. From this space situations are handled with greater ease and success. Life is less overwhelming and has greater flow as we glide around obstacles rather than allowing them to stop us in our tracks.

Some practices that encourage me to stay mindful, optimistic, reflective and appreciative are as follows:

    Unsubscribe and limit emails that don't enhance my living.
    Start the day with gratitude and positive intentions.

Challenge my existing beliefs and be curious.
Be fully present when listening, without attempting to control or judge.
Take mini-breaks when working or studying.
Indulge in random acts of kindness.
Exercise and eat mindfully.
Create a sanctuary at home.
Check my self-talk.
Be present in my relationships.
Have some reiki.
Meditate.
Breathe deeply whenever I think about it, especially during times of stress.

Affirmation

*I participate in life without judgement.
I notice and observe what is occurring around me from my calm inner space.*

> **My tip for your path to peace**
>
> Quieting, mindful moments add flow and ease to our lives as we train our minds to function from peace as our natural state. Connect with your breath and breathe into your heart space: peace resides here.

The essence

Mindfulness is a way of being that we can work towards daily, one step at a time. It occurs through consistent choices and practices to quieten our overactive and judgemental minds.

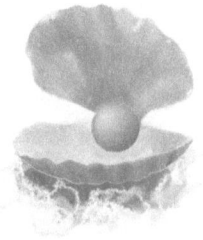

Mistakes

'OUR MISTAKES ARE MEANT TO GUIDE US, NOT DEFINE US.'

We readily embrace the 'flaws and imperfections' of others but judge ourselves harshly for things we perceive we've said or done wrong. We aren't perfect and nor do we need to be. Earth is a type of boot camp where we train and learn daily in order to get into our best shape! It's our job to make mistakes so that we can reflect, learn and grow. Trust that mistakes are all part of getting us to where we are now. Mistakes are part of our guidance system but shouldn't define or impact our essence.

If you've made a mistake that has affected someone else then make amends where possible, forgive yourself and move forwards. Guilt doesn't allow the space for change. Guilt keeps us trapped in a space of limitation and encourages self-doubt and feelings of low self-worth. Guilt is another form of fear and is a low vibration energy. Raise your vibration by reminding yourself that you would probably have no need to be on earth if you were perfect. You came here to heal and grow, and each time this occurs, those around you learn too.

Sometimes experiencing what we don't want to be or have makes it possible to perceive how we'd truly like to be and live. Life on planet Earth involves risks and trial and error. It demonstrates what is in alignment with us and what is not. It's how we change trajectory; and reflect on various attributes that may be limiting us, and perhaps no longer serving us, our lives or our relationships.

What would your life be like if you trusted there were no mistakes and you were always being guided?

Affirmation

My mistakes are friendly guides showing me what traits and behaviours I wish to discard for my highest good.

My tip for your path to peace

When you perceive you've made a mistake, breathe, breathe, breathe. Be kind to yourself and make a commitment to do better next time. Choose peaceful, nurturing thoughts and feelings.

The essence

Befriend your mistakes. They reflect for us what needs to change for our own growth and healing. Mistakes show us who we want to be and how we wish to function. They help us to uncover the best version of ourselves—if we are honest and true to ourselves.

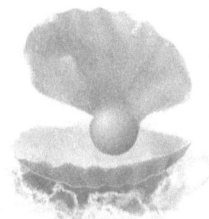

Mystical experiences

THERE EXISTS A BENEVOLENT, MAGICAL, MIRACULOUS FORCE THAT OPENS FOR US, ALLOWING US TO DELVE INTO THE UNKNOWN REALMS OF POSSIBILITY.

Be willing to be mystified, to be in awe of life, if you would like to open to the mystical in your world. Being 'mystified' is directly related to our ability to connect with and believe in something greater, something more magical, something beyond our current human functioning. Observe the wonder of nature: the patterns in the clouds, the migration of birds, the uniqueness of a snowflake, the majesty and power of an eagle in flight. Be in a receptive state of receiving the mystical, so that these types of events can escalate in a beautiful way throughout your days.

The idea of mystical experiences has always intrigued and excited me. Mystical events in my experience are filled with wonder and awe, combined with a magical shake-up, wake-up feeling that is so powerful that we can suspend disbelief, even if just momentarily. The mystical often arises without a logical explanation, and as a result can often be disregarded.

I believe that when we were children, mystical experiences existed as part of our reality, often blurred with the fantasy worlds that we created as part of our childlike belief in magic and enchantment. I was always told I had an extremely vivid imagination. I see clearly now that at times I was seeing into other realms. As we grew older these experiences were often discounted as make-believe. We then shut down these abilities and experiences as they were not validated or accepted.

I am fascinated by the stories I've heard of mystical experiences and by my own experiences. I anticipate that as we evolve even further on our spiritual journeys (and open more fully to our gifts and abilities) that these experiences will reveal themselves more frequently.

Mystical experiences in my view are the 'call' that we are receiving to step towards something greater, to reach into the unknown beyond the current reality that we see and experience. We need to be open to and accepting of these experiences in order to receive them; the universe doesn't give us what we can't handle. As we grow in wisdom, peace and enlightenment, stepping more fully into our potential, the doorway to the mystical will open. Clearing issues in our lower chakras helps us to develop greater power in the upper chakras where mystical experiences can be accessed and experienced.

For many of us the doorway to the unknown mystical realm is opening through our 'clairs', which are our psychic abilities. My dominant clairs are clairvoyance, clairaudience, clairsentience and claircognisance. Clear and balanced chakras help us to access our clairs.

Clairvoyance means clear seeing. This is when images flash into our mind. These visions can be from the past, present or future. For me, the pictures I see are then accompanied by words and a 'knowing' that gives more information. This has been amazing in my reiki, coaching/counselling and spiritual teaching business. Clairvoyance helps us find what is going on under the surface in order to gain insight and move forward, freeing clients of limitations throughout the process.

Clairaudience means clear hearing. This is when we hear words, phrases, sentences, sounds or music in our own mind. It sounds like we are hearing our own voice. Clairaudience has been a wonderful gift for my writing.

Clairsentience means clear feeling. This involves our empathic abilities: feeling someone's emotions, energy or physical symptoms. It is our gut instinct, the lightness or heaviness in our stomach or heart, and the chills and goosebumps that indicate we 'know'. Being highly sensitive and in tune with our own feelings and reactions (along with those of others) allows us to facilitate the healing process as we more readily perceive stuck energies.

Claircognisance means clear knowing. For me it's 'knowing what I know' intuitively without having prior knowledge of particular people, situations and events. There is a strong sense of an undeniable truth that comes through, seemingly out of nowhere. It can be related to the past, present or future. This is a wonderful gift, as it is a shortcut to the truth.

The mystical realm is also opening through abilities and experiences unique to each individual. One standout example of this for me was when I pulled out from a side street and didn't see a car coming from another angle. We hit, I felt the impact, saw the angry faces of the people in the other car and decided, 'No! This wasn't happening!' When I got out of the car to apologise and inspect the damage, the two cars were not touching and there was not a scratch on either car. The passengers in the car I 'hit' were too stunned to speak and got in their car and drove away. They had no words and I could tell they could not process what had just happened. I, on the other hand, knew something totally out of the ordinary had happened.

Other mystical, unexplainable experiences have happened when I've lost precious objects. An earring may be lost and then it will appear sometime later out in the open in a place it couldn't have previously been without it being seen. A family member previously witnessed this phenomenon with me. This person phoned me one day with a strange request. She said, 'I know I make fun of all this weird stuff you do and talk about, but I've lost the diamond out of my ring, I've searched for hours and I'm desperate. If you can make it appear, I'll never doubt you again.' Anyway, whether it was her belief and willingness or mine, two minutes later she said, 'OMG, the diamond is sitting next to me on the bed'.

It's always easy to put these things down to a random fluke or just an oversight. From my experience, the more we open to 'all things are possible' as our reality, the more the mystical and magical shows up!

I've also had the uncanny experience of having telepathic conversations with a few individuals who have a correlating gift from places far away from my home. Related to telepathy, I know many of us have had the experience of saying something and in turn our companion then says, 'You just plucked that thought out of my head'.

Mystical experiences often occur for me in my dreams through the experience of unusually strong energies. In one dream I was being drawn into a galaxy of stars and heard, 'don't resist'. As I let go and went with the flow, I was swept into a vortex of energy. I experienced unimaginable peace for several hours afterwards and felt like I was free of something I couldn't name.

Another time during a dream, it seemed like I was healing old wounds as I was speaking to my inner child, a younger version of myself. She was content, and the connection changed how I felt throughout the day and beyond.

The experience of connecting deeply with those I love in my dreams makes me feel uplifted and inspired in my waking hours. The power of these connections seems amplified in dreams, and the contact is often accompanied by new impressions and insights.

One of my most beautiful and gratitude inspiring mystical experiences was when I was given the sad news that my dad had a type of blood cancer that would allow him only five years to live. Once again, it was a 'that's not happening' moment, which I'm convinced is a way to access the mystical world. When we make a demand on ourselves to experience (and be something greater), we open the door to the infinite possibilities of the universe. When embracing this realm of possibility, we are almost denying that the current reality exists, and this allows us to step into a mystical, magical reality. Moving forward, I did some energy healing work on Dad, combined with the power of extreme love and intention. The following week when he went to have further tests done to determine the medical procedures to follow, there was no sign of the cancer—and over a decade later there is still no evidence of it. If one was a sceptic one could say, 'the tests must have been wrong', but I'm of the Dr Wayne Dyer school of thought, 'You will see it when you believe it'. Dad and I believe we somehow created a kind of mystical healing and it's not the only time we've created such a scene.

Affirmation

*I open the door to mystical experiences
to help me step even further
into my healing and potential.*

> ### My tip for your path to peace
>
> Peacefully embrace the mystical as it enters your life. Mystical experiences draw us intensely into the present moment—where peace exists. Trust that the benevolent conscious universe will only deliver what you can handle.

The essence

As we evolve and step further into our gifts, talents and abilities, the space will be created for the mystical to enter our lives. These experiences will further expand our consciousness and power as spiritual beings.

Nature

ACCESS THE DIVINE THROUGH NATURE.

Be nurtured by nature. The energy nature provides is healing to our mind and senses. Make time in every day to observe, admire and appreciate the gifts of nature. Watch the joy and peace gently flow through your life as you invoke this connection.

Nature is our muse. It is the source of great inspiration and creativity. My best writing arrives after spending time in nature. Be inspired by the sounds of birds chatting. Be mesmerised by the ducks landing on the water. Be entranced by the mist rolling through the valley. Be hypnotised by the rain resounding on the roof. Be in awe of the flowers in bloom turning their heads to the sun. Be recharged by the waves pounding in full force onto the beach. Be in a space of gratitude as the sun sets in a brilliant show of pinks, reds, blues and oranges. Just *be*.

Be willing to see heaven on earth, for it abounds for those who are willing to see. Our mood elevates as soon as we notice the beauty that surrounds us in nature. Nature wants to be admired so she can give us her energy. Once we connect to beauty it shows up for us everywhere, just waiting to be noticed.

Ground your scattered energies regularly by walking barefoot on the earth. Feel the calm enter your body as the build-up of daily energies is kindly dissipated by Mother Earth. Allow the sun to recharge your energies, the wind to clear negativity, and the rain to cleanse you emotionally. Let the beauty of nature inspire you to co-create and connect with the infinite possibilities of the universe. What can you truly see and feel in nature today?

We can learn a lot by observing nature. Just as trees let go of their leaves in autumn, we can be inspired to let some things go too. Perhaps it's stress. Maybe it's the less than positive stories we tell ourselves that can become our reality. Maybe it's not seeing our own beauty, worth and potential. It could be resistance to taking a leap of faith into creating something we desire. Challenge yourself to let go of limitations to your peace, happiness, wellbeing and wisdom. Keeping our stuff keeps us trapped.

Spring is about growth and change. As in nature, as it is for us. Is a new direction or a more inspired way of approaching life calling to you? Spring is about renewal and is a great time to clear the clutter physically and mentally. Clear unwanted emotions, energies and unfinished business to be able to move more positively through life. Feel the freedom as you make way for better things. Be in a renewed space and set new intentions for the upcoming months.

Affirmation

I am open to receiving the gifts, learning and inspiration that is abundant in nature.

My tip for your path to peace

Spend long enough in nature and you will know peace without effort: a peace that soothes and grounds us, a peace that radiates outward to touch our lives and relationships.

The essence

Open your connection to nature. Make time every day to listen to her whispers and she will lead your heart in the same direction your angels are guiding you: towards heaven on earth. Nature soothes our souls.

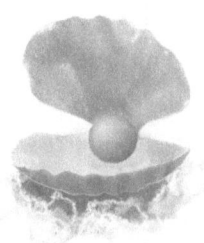

Openness to receiving

THE UNIVERSE WANTS TO GIVE TO
US OUR HEART'S DESIRES.

Receiving involves trusting that what we require, and desire is always on its way to us. It's about gratitude for where we are right now and at the same time being in a state of receptive anticipation of the unexpected. If you've asked for something to show up in your life, stay alert to what the universe presents to you. Be prepared to act, to further embrace infinite receiving. Receiving is the opposite of control. Control often means we feel like we need to manipulate outcomes, fight, compete and incessantly claw our way to make something happen. We attempt to micro-manage every facet with the attitude that there is never enough to go around. If we don't seek to control situations or people, there can be no adverse reactions when things don't go to our plan.

An example of 'ask and receive' in my life was when I wrote a letter to the universe asking for an amazing life partner to show up. I wrote down approximately twelve qualities that would be 'within' my ideal man and then let it be. It took the universe a little bit of time (a human construct) and for me to be in such a state of receiving (approximately six years, but who's counting?) for my beautiful man with all twelve criteria (and then some) to enter my life. To my amazement, my final request was for a 'whole man', someone who was complete in himself that I would not feel compelled to attempt to save or fix. His surname is Holman! The universe, combined with the individual power of surrendering control to a greater power, allowed me to know that what we can receive is truly phenomenal and beyond the realms of our imagination. True receiving allows us to be free of the limitations of the ego. Our belief is too strong for the machinations of the ego to come into play.

Our ability to receive is often based on what we perceive we deserve and is linked to our self-worth. We have to believe we are worthy of receiving what we desire. The higher our self-worth, the more likely we are to attract situations, people and circumstances that enhance our lives, and at the same time to develop the confidence to reach for our dreams. Money is a form of receiving. The more we value ourselves and are willing to receive the abundance of life, the more money flows. Be your greatest 'uplifter' today and every day.

Receiving is also connected to the stories we tell ourselves around what is impossible and possible for us. Change your stories to extraordinary ones and watch your ability to receive blossom in unexpected ways. What we put out into the universe with our thoughts, energy and emotions always comes back to us—the universe says 'yes' to all that we energetically send out. If our thoughts, energy and emotions aren't in alignment with what we are desiring to attract into our lives, it can be a very long process with less flow.

For most of us giving is easier than receiving. Both are part of the same package and are equally important to our wellbeing. Start small when developing your ability to receive, by graciously allowing others the joy of giving to you with compliments or kind deeds. Gratitude, appreciation, fun and joy raise our vibration and therefore our ability to receive.

Affirmation

I am open to receiving all that I dream of and beyond that, every day.

My tip for your path to peace

We need to embrace having no resistance to what is, or what is to come. From this space peace reigns freely as we are functioning from greater presence and less control.

The essence

The universe says 'yes' to everything we desire that serves our highest good. Our work is to believe we are worthy and to be in alignment with high vibrational energies, the true place of receiving.

Patience

AS YOU SOW, SO SHALL YOU REAP, IN THE UNIVERSE'S TIME.

Patient people give off an energy of peace and flow, as they know that everything happens at the right time. They are present and aligned with their higher selves. There is space around them for miracles as they are not obsessed with manipulating or forcing results. They trust and are not vested in specific outcomes. They have faith in themselves and their connection with the universe. They know that what they desire is on its way to them in a form that is the best match for them.

If you are inspired and approaching life with joy and intent, then what you are desiring will eventually make its way to you—if it's for your highest good and it matches your vibration. What we put out into the universe comes back to us in some form. This means we need to be an energetic match for what we desire. If not, it may take change on our part before it can show up in our life. What arrives may not look like what we initially envisaged, as something even better may show up for us.

We are limited by our imaginations, whereas the infinite, abundant universe is not. Expect amazingly wonderful things to come your way, applying patience as your dominant mode of operation. Remember we are supported and cared for by the universe, so trust this always. It might take a day, a year or a lifetime but what's meant to be yours, will always find its way to you. Enjoy the time 'in between' as you wait for what is destined for you to reveal itself in universal time, not necessarily our desired time.

Practise patience, having the willingness to learn and take the steps required, as you prepare to be in that place ready to receive a dream or two coming to fruition.

Embrace the mystery of life. Nothing is as it seems when we are creating our lives. Just like an iceberg or seeds beneath the ground, we cannot see what is going on under the surface. What we are hoping for may not have revealed itself to us yet, but powerful forces are at work on our behalf behind the scenes.

> 'When I am patient, I let the universe do for me what I cannot do for myself.'
> GABRIELLE BERNSTEIN

Sometimes it's okay (and even beneficial) to have no idea what we're doing or where we're going. Embrace the sense of freedom and the space for new possibilities that can arise from not knowing or seeking immediate answers or needing to control outcomes. Practise patience and trust while enjoying time to just 'be' or rejuvenate. Appreciate what is and at the same time excitedly await what is on its way. As the Zen proverb invites, in the meantime patiently 'chop wood and carry water'.

Affirmation

What I desire and require for my highest good is always on its way to me, in divine timing and in a way that's just right for me.

My tip for your path to peace

We don't have control over the events in our lives (even if we think we do) but we do have choice over the thoughts we focus on. Choose patient thinking that will lead you back to inner peace repeatedly. Peace in our lives begins within.

The essence

Patience is the willingness to grow, learn, change and shift anything that is in the way of creating what we require and desire in life. This occurs in a timeframe that cannot be forced by us but is instead delivered in universal time. Patient people are peaceful people as they trust that what is meant for them is on its way.

Peace

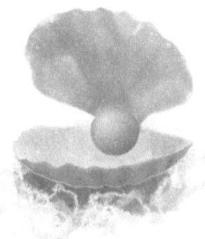

PEACE IS THE PLATFORM FROM WHICH WE BUILD POWER AND HAPPINESS.

Peace is our guide, our barometer. In the beginning of our journey to peace, before our repeated efforts to maintain it have made it our natural state, peace is as unpredictable as the weather. Choosing peace is a muscle to flex daily if we want it to become our go-to default system. Maintaining peace is our priority, the essential ingredient for creating a fulfilling life. Peace is letting go. It is remembering we are spiritual beings and reconnecting with and surrendering to our vast source of divine assistance. Peace is embracing the unknown and accepting what life presents in any given moment. It is acknowledging that we are guided and loved. It is deeply trusting in ourselves and in the flow of our lives. Peace and stillness are not empty; they contain our power, potential and wisdom.

Seeking peace helps us to truly get to know ourselves. To do this we need to be extremely honest with ourselves, noticing our reactions and learning what they reveal about how we are functioning. The ego detests peace, as peace challenges its very survival. Through quieting the voice of the ego, we build our personal power as we are no longer the puppet, nor the effect of the ego's machinations. With commitment, intention and awareness we gradually change our reactive state to one of balance, harmony and peace.

Even fleeting moments of peace bring clarity. Peace reveals to us where we are at in any given moment. If we are not experiencing ease, then we have reacted to something or someone and it is lowering our feel-good vibration. A lack of peace is our alarm system. It is calling us to wake up and receive what is going on with our emotional state. We need to look within to truthfully identify what is triggering us to not feel ease. We need to acknowledge and release our fears to get to peace. Embracing love and all its derivatives—compassion, nurturing, self-care, appreciation and gratitude—is essential for peace to reign. We need to access that place of peace inside us that is unaffected by the external world. The stronger it is the more we can weather the storms of life. If we make peace the focus for our lives, then external events have less impact as we can always choose peace regardless.

Sometimes our lives are chaotic. From chaos, new creations, new perspectives, growth and change can arise. We need to be okay with upheaval, and at the same time work to bring peace to times of duress. During turbulent times, we all have the power to manage our thoughts and corresponding emotional response. Reach for better-feeling, calming emotions to create peace within. Rise above any storms and create your own version of sunshine.

> 'Peace doesn't necessarily mean being in a place where there's no noise or trouble, rather it means that in the midst of turmoil, you can still feel calm.'
>
> Dr Wayne Dyer

Peaceful lives arise when we are content with who we are, what we are doing and where we are heading. Seek inspiration to create a life of meaning and purpose. Hold wonderful visions for your future. Fulfilling dreams equals happiness and greater peace.

Inside us all there is a place of peace, if we can stay quiet and calm enough to access it. For me, connecting to my heart space is a direct path to peace. Breathing into this space and visualising colours and images associated with love and peace, and then generating feelings associated with love and peace, help restore balance and calm.

Peace brings a clear mind where we can connect to our intuition and make choices and decisions that move us forward towards happiness and joy. Seek practices that promote calm and peace. Dive deeply into your calming self-care toolkit. Quieting moments create a calmer nervous system which changes our lives.

If you are sensitive to the energies of others, develop clear, strong boundaries, as taking on stuff for others is the antithesis of peace.

Peace is embracing the unknown. It is trusting in ourselves and in our lives so beautifully that we know we are always taken care of. We can just be with what life presents.

Affirmation

I seek peaceful thoughts and peaceful moments in all situations. Peace is my natural state. It is easy for me to experience peace.

My tip for your path to peace

Acknowledge how you are feeling with deep honesty. Release the judgement you have around your thought or emotion. Reach for thoughts that bring you back to a peaceful state, one thought at a time. Know what brings calmness to your soul. Make sure you access your toolkit, to start each day feeling calm. Before sleep, release the day.

The essence

Peace is the guide and the place through which we access our power and ensuing happiness. It is only from a state of peace that we can connect to our intuition and hear the whispers of our soul guiding us forward on our life purpose. If we are not feeling peace, there is something we need to address within: something where we have reacted, judged or chosen fear. We have moved away from our true self, our spiritual essence, and let the ego take over our thoughts and reactions. The solutions for maintaining peace are never in the outside world; they always arise from the inner world.

Pedestals

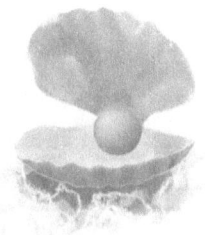

THE ONLY PERSON THAT SHOULD BE PUT ON A PEDESTAL IS YOURSELF, AS YOU ARE DOING THE BEST YOU CAN WITH THE TOOLS YOU HAVE.

We need to be cautious of putting anyone on a pedestal. It is okay for us to admire others and even to aspire to embrace some of their qualities. We can be inspired by the way others conduct their lives and use their example to reach for more of our own greatness. There are wonderful people out there to inspire and support us in our endeavours. Another person's success or amazing attributes never mean we can't be or have that too. See it all as a gift revealing what we'd like to add to our own repertoire. Avoid deciding that because someone else is doing it or being it, we can't. Comparison and lack are low vibrational states and are the opposite of attracting in what we truly desire.

Avoid giving your power to others by making them greater than you. Listen to advice (take what works for you) and seek support, but always trust your own intuition. All the answers are within us. Work on developing and finding your own power. Access your power by encouragement and kindness to self: from here your self-worth can flourish. Healthy self-esteem is an essential component, the foundation for cultivating our personal power.

Caution is required if we make the judgement that we could never be that amazing, that loving, that aware, that talented, that gifted, that rich and so on. This approach limits what we can achieve or aspire to, as we may have already decided that there are things we can't have or be. It promotes low self-worth and suffering by comparison.

The person you admire and have 'pedestalled' can become highly intimidating for you to be around. Sometimes you may not feel good enough when in their presence. Putting people on pedestals encourages the ego part of our minds to start looking for faults. This means judging them and eventually even deciding we don't like them. This is the only way we may feel comfortable to be around them as our ego insists on finding some 'flaws'. Our reactions and judgements can invoke the tall poppy syndrome: trying to cut someone down so we can feel okay in their presence. When we are in this space, we attempt to take them off the pedestal they never asked to be on, and we separate from them. None of us are perfect. Instead, remember that everyone is on their own journey and even people we've put on pedestals have their challenges to overcome.

If you admire qualities in someone, there is a fair chance they are mirroring attributes that you already have but are unwilling (as yet) to acknowledge. You may be only one or two steps behind. Ask them questions about their journey. See what you can learn to further assist you stepping into being the best version of yourself. There are qualities you may aspire to emulate, but at the same time appreciate and have gratitude for where you are at. Develop a sense of wonder about where you are heading and who you are stepping into being.

Affirmation

I look at people I admire with the view to develop these qualities (and more) within me. I allow myself to perceive and reveal my own uniquely wonderful attributes for the world to see.

> ### My tip for your path to peace
>
> There is peace to be found in being the best version of you and in trusting that no-one is any better or worse than you. We are all at uniquely and equally important stages of our journey.

The essence

We are all on our own journeys with our own issues and 'situations' to overcome. Allowing and appreciating the light that others shine assists us to cultivate and appreciate our own.

Perfectionism

LOW SELF-WORTH IN DISGUISE.
HEAL IT AND ALL WILL FLOURISH.

We are all a work in progress. We need to appreciate our individual time frame for growth. It is essential that we honour the learning experiences that are presented to us in life. Avoid harsh self-judgement (regarding desired or undesired outcomes) to consistently nurture our self-esteem and negate the need for obsessive perfectionism.

Perfectionism can be both a fear of failure and a way of protecting fragile self-worth. Perfectionism can be fuelled by a fear of judgement from ourselves and more often from others. We convince ourselves that if we do enough perfectly, we can be okay. Doing things 'beyond better' makes us feel safer as we presume we will be less likely to receive negative judgement. To get free of perfectionism (that is overwhelming and controlling) we need to nurture our self-worth. We need to be our own advocate, our own life coach, our own biggest supporter. Using kind words and thoughts that lift us up rather than knock us down is key. We need to watch our thoughts and stop the critical voice before it has an impact.

Perfectionism can feel like a freight train running through us. It is a high-adrenaline way of functioning and is the opposite of peace. Rather than constantly looking at an overly ambitious 'to do' list, we need to simplify it. Do less, better, and with greater peace and calm. Allowing more space in the day for calm and stillness helps with flow and creativity. From here we can achieve wonderful things more easily and successfully.

We need to trust that we are 'imperfectly perfect'. Being imperfect allows us to connect with others as we bond over mutual challenges and common experiences; from here we can share our insight with others. We lose sight of who we are and diminish our ability to gain self-knowledge and connect to our intuition when we are focused on being perfect. If we were perfect, there would be no need and therefore no space for growth and learning. If we decide we are perfection personified, then we will be less inclined to seek change. Change is essential for inspiration and creativity to flourish. All things in life are in flux, as are we. We are on planet Earth to grow, learn and heal. Any perceived imperfections or mistakes are gifts and guides in disguise.

Affirmation

*I am always in the right place at the right time.
I am doing exactly what needs to be done for both success and my highest good.*

> **My tip for your path to peace**
>
> Create from a space of calm and kindness to self and have realistic expectations in all situations. Be at peace being the imperfectly perfect creation you truly are.

The essence

Relax. Rome wasn't built in a day. Quality is produced when we allow significant time to create and to learn from our mistakes. At the same time, it is essential to nurture and build ourselves up, to establish effective flow and productivity.

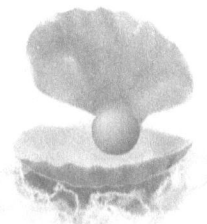

Possibilities

BEYOND OUR IMAGINATION …
AND CONTROL.

Possibilities are the light in life, the inspiration, the excitement. Possibilities are as necessary for us as the air we breathe and the water that replenishes us. Each day if we are truly living, we are reaching for the stars on so many levels, even if it's unacknowledged. We are aiming for a big life, a life filled with surprises and miracles that take us in new directions chosen specifically for us. Possibility is the antithesis of boredom and depression. Possibilities create spark and potential within us.

Being connected to our higher self and staying in alignment with our divine source are essential ingredients for being in the space to know when to act on possibility. Possibility is linked directly with intuition. As possibilities reveal themselves, we need to be able to hear our inner voice to respond to the call. We may find ourselves meeting someone unexpected or being in the right place at the right time for an opportunity to present itself, or for a new door to open.

Possibility might come in the form of a seed of inspiration that ignites a desire to write a book or a poetry collection. It could be the desire to form new connections, improve our existing relationships or dream of a love we hadn't previously thought possible. It might be the desire to radically change careers or take a giant leap of faith and create a business. It might show up in the form of being 'discovered' and being taken on a new path to a new destiny. On another day it may show up as a desire to visit the most beautiful places on the planet or to beautify your own surroundings. Next week it could be time to learn something new: dancing, flying a kite, paddle-boarding, cooking exotic dishes or white-water rafting.

Possibilities catapult us from the mundane into the extraordinary. Dream a little or a lot every day and feel deep within what new possibilities may be stirring. Opening the door to change and new possibilities propels us forward in life and brings a richness of experience to our lives.

Affirmation

My life is an ever-expanding force of unlimited possibilities.

My tip for your path to peace

Flow where life and your intuition are taking you. Peace is taking the path of least resistance into possibility.

The essence

Being open to amazing possibilities is our divine birthright. Possibilities will be presented to us throughout every step and stage of life. We need to be present and open to be able to see and act upon them.

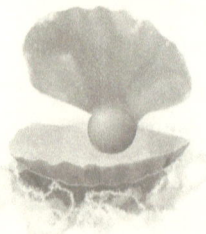

Power

POWER IS WHAT AND WHO WE ARE WHEN WE ARE ALIGNED WITH OUR TRUE SELF AND OUR DIVINE SOURCE.

Power and control struggle to live side by side. We need to decide whether we would rather function from control or power. Control is ego-driven and is about wanting things to turn out exactly as we've decided they should, being focused purely on the external world and reacting when things don't go as planned. There is no surrender to our higher power when doing control. Control limits possibilities as we are only accessing our human self, not our divine higher self.

Power is something that arises from within when we are connected to our divine nature and source. When we access our power, we know we will be okay with no matter what comes our way. From that space true receiving can occur, as we are present and allowing life to show up in a way that serves our highest good. We accept what is and know that creative solutions and new possibilities are always available.

Being powerful means accessing our whole self (our strengths and abilities) and using our gifts with intention, love and compassion.

Looking within, identifying and getting free of our shadow aspects builds personal power. We don't need to be saved or rescued but we do need to process our past and heal our wounds so we can step into our light and power. Self-care, self-knowledge and self-worth are key ingredients in allowing our power to bloom and flourish. Having faith and trust in ourselves and in the path that is unfolding for us builds our power; self-doubt undermines us. Power is knowing who you are, what doesn't serve you and what lights you up. It is letting go of all that limits you and allowing in that which needs to come. Being in our power allows us respect and appreciate ourselves (without judgement) and to grow, learn and step into our full potential.

Accessing our power brings us closer to living the life of our dreams as there is nothing in our way. We are the only ones powerful enough to block our own dreams. We need to acknowledge our own power and take the necessary steps to access it. Personal power is linked directly to our ability to create, seek and accept change. What would you like to change today and what else is possible for you and your life?

We need to avoid giving our power away by making ourselves 'less than' in the face of others. We are all equal and on different stages of our journey. We all lose our power in different ways: judgement, comparison, envy, worrying, lack of self-care, seeking approval and having unclear boundaries are some of the most obvious ways. Calling back our power becomes easier the more we recognise when and how it is leaking from us. What is required to replenish our power will vary from day to day depending on our current self-care needs. For me, identifying and discussing feelings as they arise, reiki, body balance, positive affirmations, being in nature and meditation help to restore my power. We are the keepers of our own wisdom. Seek help and advice but always trust your own intuition and choose what feels right for you. Make decisions for your highest good.

A special note for empaths: be aware of narcissists. Our light, inner strength, combined with our desire to heal wounds and our forgiving natures, makes us magnets for narcissists. Narcissists seek to own and control our power as they don't have their own inner reservoir, despite their often outward charismatic and confident personas. They are masters of manipulation and illusion. They do not like it if we shine brighter than they do and will do what they can to get us to give away our power. In their presence we often feel somewhat diminished or anxious, with a feeling of something not being quite right. Narcissists are great at manipulating us to feel self-doubt or wrongness, which diminishes our power. In the past (and I'm so glad I can say 'in the past') potential narcissistic relationships began as me being in equal measure both incredibly attracted and repelled by the narcissist who was currently presenting himself. When facing a narcissist, it is imperative that we stand in our power and know when to 'move away' and take a different path.

Affirmation

I seek my own power through self-awareness, self-care, divine connection and strong boundaries. I move through life knowing I am powerful beyond measure and act accordingly.

> **My tip for your path to peace**
>
> Avoid playing small. The resistance you need to apply, to limit your own power, is the opposite of peace.

The essence

Stepping into our power means we are moving further away from self-imposed limitations and closer to our greatness and all that we came here to be. Our lives will be blessed with greater purpose and meaning when we live as our most powerful selves.

Questions

MAKE SURE THE UNIVERSE HEARS YOU, OFTEN.

Life changes when we begin to live in a state of question: that is, communicating daily our desires to the divine, God, universe, angels, ascended masters, guides, source (whatever it is for you). The universe celebrates as each person connects on a deeper level or actively makes contact for the first time. We have a heavenly team that waits patiently for us to ask. As it is a free-will universe, we need to ask to receive guidance and assistance. Questions open us to infinite possibilities and bring an expansive energy to our lives.

Practise asking questions of the universe each day. Anticipate guidance in universal time (not our time) and be patient. Much may need to occur for your 'team' to answer your call and to facilitate bringing your desires into this reality.

You might ask:
> What would it take for a career that is fun, nurturing and generative to come into my life?

What would it take for a nurturing partner to come into my life, someone who is going to help me step into being the best I can be?
What is it going to take for my body and me to enjoy optimal health?
What would it take for (..........) or something even greater to show up for me?

Next, gently let these questions go on the wings of angels. Release expectations as to the way your questions will receive a response. Think big and then allow the universe to work its magic. Often something even better than we can imagine for meeting our needs (for our highest good) will show up.

Asking questions helps us co-create our reality with universal assistance and guidance. It helps our choices to be in alignment with who we are and where we are heading. Be free of conditions regarding time when asking for divine assistance. The universe doesn't respond to time as we do. Patience is necessary. It means we are willing to observe, listen, take the necessary steps and act when appropriate in order to realise a new dream or desire manifesting for us.

Affirmation

I co-create a reality beyond my wildest dreams with constant divine connection and assistance. I ask and I receive.

> ### My tip for your path to peace
>
> A sense of peace comes by actively seeking connection with our divine source through our questions as we sense we are being heard, guided and assisted. We can then peacefully flow; trusting in life.

The essence

Questions provide direct access to universal wisdom and inspiration. We live in a space that is open to receiving guidance. We are not having to do everything on our own, as we have the universe as our partner throughout life.

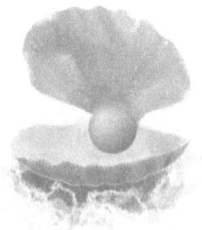

Reiki

A BEAUTIFUL GIFT TO OURSELVES AND THE PLANET.

Just as we have the body systems, we have an energy system that underpins our spiritual, physical, emotional and mental health. Energy medicine is fast gaining popularity as an answer to health for the future. Unlike pharmaceutical drugs, there are no adverse side-effects. Reiki is tailored to meet current needs for increasing wellbeing and potential. Reiki does what it needs to do (in the moment) for a person to continue moving forward spiritually, emotionally, mentally and physically. Reiki and other forms of energy healing are so effective because they can bypass the ego to heal from within.

There are few experiences that come close to having one's chakras cleared, balanced and revitalised. Keeping our chakras clear and balanced through reiki allows us to trust ourselves, step into our power and follow our intuition. We clear our own issues and those we've absorbed from others. This helps our mind, emotions and physical body to work together in harmony.

Even the smallest energetic shift is enough to open new doors in career, relationships, diet and lifestyle. Each session brings forms of enlightenment, change and growth—even if one is not initially aware of it. Reiki promotes greater self-knowledge, which is one of the hardest and most life-changing things to master.

Clients often experience a sense of peace and lightness, increased confidence and awareness, freedom from long-term emotional patterns, easing of physical ailments and a greater ability to forgive, let go and move forward. Many start to give themselves permission to feel good, appreciating and knowing that's what they deserve. Life flows with more abundance and ease. Challenges are met with greater strength, and problems often dissolve into solutions. Miraculous moments and synchronicity occur more frequently. Many reiki clients have learnt to expect the unexpected and to relish it.

Energy healing is for you if you wish to:

- protect your energetic boundaries
- feel peace and calm
- feel grounded
- improve connections with others
- enhance creativity
- feel lighter and more joyful
- be loving towards yourself and others
- be able to clearly speak your truth
- listen to your intuition and connect to divine guidance
- step into your power and potential.

Receive the gift of reiki and watch change occur in subtle, yet powerful and pervasive ways. It is like dropping a pebble in a pond. The ripple effect magnifies and who knows how far-reaching its effects will be.

If you wish to step into being the best version of yourself, place yourself on a reiki 'diet'. As you change, you energetically influence and change those around you in a positive way, on some level. Be the gift that changes the lives of others and heals the planet; all is made possible through the experience of reiki.

> 'The true purpose of reiki is to correct the heart and mind;
> keep the body healthy; and lead a happy life using
> the spiritual capabilities we've been
> endowed with since birth.'
>
> MIKAO USUI

Affirmation

*I am willing to receive healing energy
to bring about the changes required
to lead me on my quest towards becoming
the best version of myself.*

My tip for your path to peace

Find an experienced, reputable reiki master and experience peace as you are meant to feel it. Reiki is peace: spiritually, emotionally, mentally and physically. One session of reiki is equivalent to a week's holiday for mind, body and spirit.

The essence

Reiki heals on all levels. It connects you to your intuition and brings awareness of what's going on under the surface, clearing emotional issues before they can trigger physical dis-ease. Reiki helps to free you of a lifetime of accumulated 'stuff' which prevents growth and healing. It clears out your 'closets' and makes space for more of you, your abilities and the awareness of possible future directions to show up.

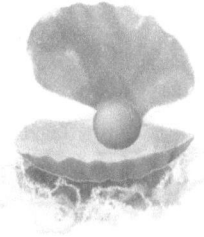

Resistance

**RESIST NOTHING,
RECEIVE EVERYTHING.**

Resistance is that heavy, sometimes frustrating and despairing energy that keeps us out of alignment with who we are and what we came here to be and achieve. Resistance takes us away from accepting the present moment as we avoid or resist what is calling to us. It can feel like having a brick weighing us down, making us feel flat and anxious, as we are not listening to our inner voice and are flowing against life rather than ebbing along with it.

Resistance keeps us where we are currently at and at the same time limits our chances of doing the great work we know in our hearts we should be doing. It often shows up as procrastination, putting off until tomorrow what we need to be doing today. If you're encountering resistance, you must be here to do wonderful things, as on the other side of resistance your greatness is waiting. Stepping into our true potential can be a little scary, as life as we know it may change. Hence we resist, as we like our comfortable but limited comfort zones.

Receiving is our gift from the heavens and allows our lives to flow with ease and abundance. If we are in resistance, we are attempting control. Control creates a space of non-receiving as we unconsciously don't allow anything to show up that does not match our limited thinking. The universe, however, is unlimited and abundant and is willing to give to us continually. Resistance can block something that is part of the divine plan for us.

On the flip side, resistance can be our own awareness and universal energy slowing us down because we are not quite prepared for what lies ahead. Trust your own instincts to know whether your resistance is procrastination or a connection with divine timing that is holding you back, preparing you to be in the right space and place to receive what is to come.

> 'Accept what comes to you woven in the pattern of your destiny, for what could more aptly fit your needs?'
> MARCUS AURELIUS

Affirmation

*I release all resistance to receiving
all that is flowing for my highest good.
I trust in divine timing and am
always in the space of receiving.*

My tip for your path to peace

Resistance is the opposite of peace. Give up resistance to what is and to what you are being called to do and be. Let go and let live.

The essence

Trust that your life is always being guided. No resistance to what life is presenting for us in the moment equals peace, flow and co-creation.

Romance

LOVE, PEACE AND PLEASURE EQUAL ROMANCE.

Romance is caring so much about another person that we tune into what makes their soul sing and their beauty shine, and we 'deliver' where possible from time to time. Romance is lighting each other up. Out of curiosity (for the male perspective) I asked my husband what romance meant to him. He promptly replied, 'It's just what you do when you are truly connected to someone and you want to make them happy'. Romance for me is a dimension of love that includes unbridled fun, newness and the anticipation of possibilities. If we are to love fully (both ourselves and others), our own cups need to be filled first; what flows over the sides can be beautifully given to another. Romance is total presence with another—we are fully immersed in what our partner is being and saying. Romance is raising each other up to new levels of inspiration through love and support. It is generating excitement for the life we are creating together. It is strengthening our relationship so much that all storms can be weathered. Romance brings peace and gratitude for our connection.

There are many 'little' things (that have huge results) that are unique to each couple, all which have the potential to re-ignite our love affair. Flowers work wonders to create romance as they are mini miracles that give light, love and inspiration to all who can see and experience them. Beautiful words, texts, cards and compliments light us up. All forms of appreciation make us feel cherished. Reminiscing over beautiful moments spent together and remembering why we first fell in love generates romance. My husband and I regularly reflect on our journey, laughing at our early history and having such appreciation for where we are now. Lighting a candle helps us to remember the light within and lights up our senses, it can smell intoxicatingly divine. Connecting with other couples who have a great connection can also be contagious—or conversely make us aware that we've got some work to do in creating our own romantic paradise. Sending songs with meaningful lyrics that remind us of our loved one can also be deeply and beautifully received. My daughter and her partner have long periods apart, and some of the songs they send each other move me to tears. Romance can be cooking a favourite meal, a thoughtfully planned date (such as an impromptu picnic), an uplifting comment, fits of laughter, a beautiful hug or a surprise adventure. Tune in and let your imagination do the rest. Celebrate love today and every day, lovers of love!

Affirmation

*I let love and intuition
lead the way to
bring myself and
my partner joy.*

My tip for your path to peace

Embrace childlike fun and (at least once) acknowledge Valentine's Day, and of course special anniversaries. You will 'receive' greater peace flowing from your partner if these auspicious occasions are recognised, honoured and enjoyed.

The essence

Tune into what makes your partner's heart sing, and deliver where possible. Your life and relationship will thank you for it.

Saying goodbye

IT IS REALLY 'BLESS YOUR JOURNEY AND SEE YOU SOON'.

Saying goodbye to loved ones can be very challenging and emotional. I've changed my dialogue around saying goodbye. It is now 'see you soon', as it creates a lighter, more expansive energy. 'See you soon' helps me to perceive the adventure and possibilities inherent in the parting. We all need to say 'goodbye' many times throughout life, to many people we care about. Saying goodbye often means we are journeying into uncharted territory and are opening to opportunities to spread our wings, grow and learn. It is all part of life on earth, life which is dedicated to reaching our full potential.

Everyone has a pathway and purpose unique to them. It is our job to support the exploration involved in each journey. A new journey should always be celebrated, even if we have mixed feelings about it. Sometimes we need to journey down pathways we may be unsure of, often to find out what we don't want. Each journey brings us closer to finding our true direction and one that lights us up.

Send those you love away with blessings. Surround them with good wishes, light and love so that the journey ahead can meet their needs and provide experiences and opportunities beyond what they can imagine. When our loved ones return, we hope they are richer from their experience. In turn, we grow and learn on some level as we are all connected. Gratitude and appreciation are wonderful states in which to live, and the parting from and return of our loved ones promotes this. When away from them, we truly know what they mean to us. We are filled with gratitude for the joy, love and inspiration they bring to our lives.

When saying goodbye, focus on the love you have for the person leaving or for the people you are leaving behind. Remember we are always connected to the ones we love energetically, if not in physical form. This will make it easier for all concerned to make the transition into being apart. Trust that each journey is blessed and that our loved ones will be safe, protected and guided.

Affirmation

I part with others on loving terms. I open to the possibilities and potential inherent in transitions and goodbyes. I trust that every journey is blessed.

My tip for your path to peace

Make sure 'all is well' upon parting and that any conversations that need to be had are conducted positively. Parting on positive and loving terms is paramount and essential for peace.

The essence

Journeys and goodbyes are a part of the tapestry of life. See the wonder, the potential for growth and the increased love and appreciation possible in each parting. Avoid holding onto loved ones too tightly. Allow them to create their own reality, make their own choices and follow their own pathway.

Self-care

SELF-CARE IS ESSENTIAL FOR BOTH SURVIVAL AND SANITY.

The only way to successfully navigate life and put our best foot forward is to prioritise self-care. If we don't make caring for ourselves a priority, who else will? When we fully care for ourselves, we have strong boundaries and an aura of self-worth around us which encourages respect and kindness from others. If we don't care for ourselves, often others 'couldn't care less' and we attract little in the way of support.

When our own cup is full (and running over) we can work miracles. We connect to our very best selves and our intuition. We are aligned with divine energies and are often unstoppable. When we are fully taking care of ourselves, we can care for others beautifully, effectively and with ease. Most importantly we are not depleting ourselves, and the care given is without detriment to us. If we give from a place of exhaustion or overwhelm, it can be less effective giving. Caring for others when we are depleted often comes with a tinge of resentment or anger, as it can be connected to an underlying 'what about me?' energy.

Many of us, particularly in the caring and healing professions, risk burnout and associated health issues due to the massive amounts of energy we give away. We need to revitalise our own energies so we can assist those who need us, without emptying our own cups and compromising our health and wellbeing. Ideally giving and receiving are most effective as simultaneous events. Balance is key.

Self-care means we are functioning from love: appreciation, gratitude, kindness, nurturing, compassion and respect for self. These qualities are cherished when they are gifted to us from others. As like attracts like, we need to direct these attributes to ourselves, before they may be forthcoming from others.

We maintain our gardens, our homes and our bodies (unless we are on a lazy patch) to keep them functioning at their best. We need to do this regular maintenance for our energy systems as well—think reiki, kinesiology and acupuncture. It is how we stay happy, healthy and attract positive people and situations into our lives. This helps to keep us moving forwards, creating new possibilities to reach greater levels of our own potential.

What would you like to do to care for yourself ... today ... tomorrow ... next week?

What might self-care look like for you?

For me, self-care is checking in with my internal peace barometer. If I'm moving too far from peace, I stop, breathe and intuitively connect to what I am feeling and experiencing. From here, I identify what I require to shift any lower vibrational energies and thinking patterns, restore my equilibrium and feel good. Simple tools and approaches are often the most effective for me. Walking barefoot on the earth or along a beach, sitting in my garden soaking up the peace and beauty, acupuncture, reiki, massage, facials, reading, yoga, swimming, sleep and meditation are all regular features of my self-care toolkit.

Review your approach to self-care regularly. Ask yourself, 'Is it still working?' If a chosen form of self-care is still effective, you will look forward to it, and it will make you feel more at peace—or more powerful, more energised, even more enlightened. Results will depend on what we aim to achieve from a session. As we change and life evolves, our self-care needs can also change. The most important thing is that we embrace self-care as an essential part of our optimal wellbeing toolkit.

> 'Self-care is a divine responsibility.'
> DANIELLE LAPORTE

Affirmation

Self-care is my gift to self.
All indulgence contributes to
my own light and energy.
I am intuitively drawn to forms
of self-care that revitalise me.

My tip for your path to peace

Develop your own peace barometer. Do whatever it takes to consistently move back to peaceful emotions and thought patterns, one step or thought at a time. Self-care is a wonderful distraction from low vibes and an excellent enhancer of healing, high vibrational and peaceful states.

The essence

Many of us take excellent care of our homes, gardens, cars and loved ones without a second thought. Self-care needs to be our first thought, our go-to way of functioning. It is essential for building healthy momentum and wellbeing as the foundation of our lives.

Self-worth

WE ARE ALL WORTHY. BELIEVE IT TO
ACCESS IT WITHIN YOURSELF.

Developing our self-worth is a lifelong process. Feelings of unworthiness hold so much more power than we realise. Our self-worth greatly determines what we will allow ourselves to have, be and experience in life. Judgement of ourselves, and also our reactions to the behaviour and opinions of others, is always tied to our self-worth. Strong self-worth allows us to deflect what doesn't serve us with far greater ease. We flow through life with greater resilience, respect and self-love.

Enhancing our self-worth is a moment-to-moment daily task. Be a detective and look for any experiences or connections with others that trigger low self-worth. Don't judge these feelings but instead use them as a guide to shine light on any old wounds that are still unhealed. Give yourself extreme compassion when confronting areas of low worth. Nurture and coach yourself until you are willing to let some of these old emotions go. Identify the patterns of thinking, behaviour and past experiences that could be limiting your self-worth and life worth.

Our outer world is generally a reflection of what is going on within. The more we strive to enhance the feelings and thoughts we allow about ourselves, the more we can step into our power and potential. We are all meant to shine! Are you willing to find out how exceptional you really are and what you're truly capable of? It's all there. We just need to lift the veil on low self-worth to reveal our greatness, so that our great worth is no longer temporarily concealed.

For me, a commitment to acknowledging that there is no 'truth' behind feelings of low worth has been key. It is the ego at work in a stealthy form. Low self-worth is an illusion, a smokescreen to prevent us from seeing and accessing our greatness. Refuse to allow it to run your existence. We must get smart to soothe our mind and spirit. It only takes a few degrees of 'shift' in our worth for our most beautiful, cherished self (which is always there) to show up in our lives.

My tips for enhancing self-worth:

Self-discovery, and removing what no longer serves us, increases our self-worth. Every time you get free of a shadow aspect within, you will feel more worth each time.

Spend your time with people that generally respect you, care for you and want the best for you.

Indulge in experiences and work that make you feel good about yourself.

Don't hang with people who are envious or jealous of you, as they will often subtly undermine you, in an attempt to feel less adequate in your presence.

Don't play small to fit in; shine your light always. You will feel anxious and unworthy if you resist being who you truly are.

Become aware of who 'emotions' belong to. It is so easy to take on thoughts, feelings and emotions for others. Ask for 'all this that's not mine' to be released to the light.

Ground yourself by walking barefoot. It will help connect you with your true essence and worth, not the form of worth that has been influenced by others around you all day.

Surrender feelings of unworthiness as they arise. Let it go, let it go.

Start the day with positive affirmations about yourself.

Meditate on your own worth.

Write in your journal (over and over) about all your positive attributes.

Practise being grateful for all that you are and all that you have. This will build the momentum of worth within you.

Replace any negative thought directed at yourself with something positive and acknowledge that you are a work in progress, always learning, changing and growing. You are not and do not ever have to be perfect.

When feelings of low worth surface do some tapping (emotional freedom technique).

All forms of self-care allow us to cherish ourselves and make us feel more like our best selves.

Laugh, stay light and don't make anything too significant.

Surround yourself with beautiful flowers and crystals—anything that lights you up.

Affirmation

*I am worthy.
I am good enough in all
situations and with all people.
I love and respect me.
I shine bright like a diamond.*

My tip for your path to peace

If you haven't quite made it to feelings of high self-worth, trust that your efforts will lead you there. Be patient. Focus on inner peace as the starting point. Peace is the foundation for feelings of happiness and worth to flourish upon.

The essence

Higher self-worth encourages us to be open to receive more joyful experiences and great opportunities because we know we deserve them.

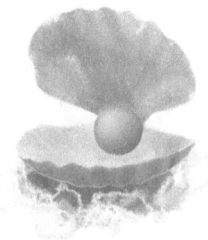

Sensuality

HEAVEN FOR THE SENSES.

Sensuality is an invitation to be joy, light and love. It implies a degree of self-love and appreciation that inspires others to step into their own radiance. We are taking care of ourselves physically and emotionally, and we exude love and self-respect. Expressing our sensuality leaves people wondering, questioning and inadvertently seeking change in the face of sensual 'inspiration'. When embracing sensuality, we can light up others just with our knowing, self-loving, confident presence. Sensual beings reflect an inner glow that can never be bought with expensive products—although it most certainly can be enhanced with all the glorious treats for the senses that are available! Cleopatra knew what she was doing when she was indulging in her milk baths. Her sensuality wasn't only beautiful, it was powerful. Sensuality allows us to connect with our power, as there is no place for self-doubt when we embrace our sensuality in totality.

Sensuality is an immediate invitation to peace, as through our sensuality we are often highly present. Sensuality leads us to connect with the beauty within ourselves, and in our lives. Appreciating our beauty is peace—we value who we are.

Our bodies love to be cherished and nurtured. Indulge your body and senses whenever you can with sunsets, beach walks, candles, baths, beautiful bedding, massages, spa treatments, facials, reiki, body lotions, perfumes and whatever is nourishing for your body and spirit. Your body will love you for it and your mind will soon catch on. A calm mind creates a relaxed, happy, healing body. A sensual demeanour softens life for those who possess it.

Sensuality attracts sensuality. Be prepared to draw in beautiful people, situations, events and treasures into your life. Be the sensual god or goddess you are truly meant to be.

Affirmation

I nourish and nurture my body to bring softness and sensuality to my life.

> **My tip for your path to peace**
>
> Invoke feelings of peace by indulging your senses in pleasurable experiences that nurture your body. Peace comes through invoking and owning our sensuality as we are being true to ourselves and proud of it.

The essence

Sensuality is the ultimate indicator of self-love and self-care. Self-love and an appreciation of one's body and spirit create a sensual presence that is an invitation for others to be in that space too.

Signs and symbols

HEAR THE GENTLE WHISPERS OF THE UNIVERSE.

We receive guidance from the universe in mysterious and magical ways as soon as we open ourselves to the possibility of such communication. Our spiritual team of guides and angels (or whatever it is for each person) await our requests for assistance and guidance. It is a free-will universe, so in order to access divine guidance we need to actively engage with this guidance.

Questions open the doorway for guidance to come into our lives as connection is instantly activated. Asking our guides of love and light for signs that we are on the right track is fun, enlightening and reassuring.

I have found that there are common signs from above along with those that are unique to some individuals. Seeing double and triple numbers has always been an indication for me that I am on the right track: 111, 222, 333, 444 and 555 are particular favourites, reminding me that all things are possible, I am guided and all is well. Combinations of 11 remind me that I am answering my calling; and that I have a continued responsibility to do so. I will often hear song lyrics and titles that relate to the current guidance I am seeking. Images and words jump out from books and magazines. Birds and animals also have a way of catching my attention and infusing me with new thinking. Clients have shared their numerous signs with me; some of the most recognisable signs are birds, white animals, rainbows, dragonflies, unicorn images, coins and butterflies.

Start with small requests for the universe (if that is the easiest way for you) to begin connecting with the guidance of signs and symbols. For example, there was a dress that I wished to buy, and it wasn't in my size. I was pondering whether or not to wait and see if it came back in stock or to choose another—yes, I know, important stuff! I asked, 'Universe, please show me a white feather within 24 hours if this dress will become available'. That afternoon, while swimming in a large resort pool, I stood up to take a rest and a white feather landed in front of me. The dress was back in stock that evening. Nearing completion of this book (when I really had no idea how to go about getting it published), I asked for the sign of a star if the book was going to find a publisher. That evening, sitting on a balcony having dinner in Darling Harbour, I glanced over my shoulder at the Ferris wheel and it had 'Star of the Show' written on the side of it. I went into a little doubt and thought maybe that was bit obvious, as this Ferris wheel is a permanent feature, so I asked for a more obvious sign. That night, I happened to turn over my journal and noticed for the first time that there were gold stars along the bottom of it. Once again, I convinced myself that this was a bit obvious because I should have noticed the stars before. So, demanding as I was, I asked again. At lunch the next day, I glanced up and saw a man walk past with a huge star on his T-shirt accompanied by the words 'The Star'. The man's stomach was very large, so this particular sign was unmissable. Clever! I was convinced at last: such was the patience of the universe.

Before submitting the title for this book, I was drawn to two titles. I asked the universe for a sign by the end of the week if the title should be 'Pearls of Wisdom: For Your Path to Peace'. That evening as I opened my novel, there were song lyrics in one of the paragraphs on that page: 'Bringing in the pearls, bringing in the pearls'.

Another time when I was feeling a little fragile, I asked the universe for a dove sign to show me if my guides were with me. I heard very clearly, 'you know we are, no sign is needed'. The universe is smart and tricky and gives us what we require, not always what we need.

If you don't get a sign it could be the universe's way of saying, 'you've got this' or 'trust yourself to make that decision'. It may mean that what you are asking for isn't ready yet—it's not yet time. Also, sometimes a sign can take a little longer to reveal itself while the universe brings the pieces of the puzzle together. Sometimes the sign will come after we've made a decision, reaffirming that we are on the right path.

Affirmation

I have a beautiful connection with my spiritual team. I readily receive clear signs in response to my communication with the universe.

> ### My tip for your path to peace
>
> Trust in universal guidance. It will bring peace to your days as you will know deeply that you are always guided and supported.

The essence

Signs are the quintessential way in which we are reminded tangibly of our divine connection and of our ability to communicate with our spiritual team.

Soulmates

LOVE IS ALL THERE IS …
THAT IS REAL.

Soulmate connections can be recognised by their instant impact. Spontaneous 'acknowledgement' could arise in the form of deep curiosity, an energetic wave of connection, lusty chemistry, a feeling of needing to run for the hills, or a combination of all scenarios. Soulmates enter our lives in the form of romantic connections, in friendships and also in seemingly unhealthy relationships and associations. Whatever the case, these connections are our teachers.

Soulmates provide ways for us to release karma and to grow. These connections can push our buttons and shine light on what we have been unwilling or unable to see within ourselves. They can be complicated and fill us with a feeling of uncertainty and often come with a hefty degree of upheaval. These often tumultuous connections are designed to heal our wounds and to release fear in all its many forms (anxiety, guilt, blame, shame) so that we can step into our true power and our potency for change.

Soulmate connections demand that we become the best version of ourselves. If this is not the case, and each individual does not heal their personal wounds, then it can be an extremely challenging relationship in which one or both soulmates are limited in reaching their true potential. The relationship will often be one of friction and unease if karma and old wounds aren't healed.

Soulmate connections can be utterly intoxicating and infuse us with an indescribable love that is so buoyant and light that it feels like anything (absolutely anything) is possible. The energy that gets created in this way is so potent that it can change all those who connect with it. From this place of healing and wholeness soulmates can create miracles for themselves and others.

I often have clients ponder the question, 'Is he/she the One?' Gosh that places a lot of pressure on the potential 'One'. The discussion always comes back to how the person makes them feel. If the relationship lights them up and they feel nurtured, supported and inspired then there is potential. In great relationships both partners are happy and feel drawn to be the best people they can be, and at the same time desire to create an inspiring, loving life together. No-one is seeking to change or control or dominate in the relationship. I've come to realise that there are often several 'Ones' along the way, which can lead to a big love when you are truly ready to receive that level of unconditional love. My advice is that we enjoy each step in the relationship, all the while growing, healing and evolving. Trust that if the relationship isn't working, it can end amicably for the highest good of all, creating the space for new love to enter at the right time.

Beyond soulmates you may want to investigate information and opinions on true mates (see the work of Cyndi Dale) and then there are twin flames …

Affirmation

*I heal me and embrace all that is required
to be the best version of myself.
I allow my soulmate(s) the space
and love required to also become whole.
Together we learn, change
and become unstoppable.*

My tip for your path to peace

See all your connections as potential 'soulmates' in order to embrace the learning, growth and love that these connections can provide. Be at peace with what transpires, trusting that these encounters are all for our highest good.

The essence

Soulmates are our partners and teachers in life. They are divinely sent to challenge us, heal us and move us forward for our highest good, and to help us step into accessing our greatest potential.

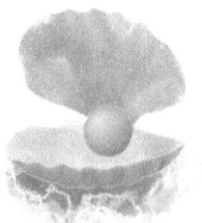

Spontaneity

WE GROW OUTSIDE THAT PLACE
WE HAVE DECIDED IS OUR
COMFORT ZONE.

Surprise and momentary freedom from the constraints of time nourish the soul. Spontaneity is a quick recharge for our spirit. It reminds us to be out of control and out of the box. In this space we can truly receive what the present moment is offering. Spontaneity sends a message to the universe that we are ready to receive, as we are open to all that the universe has to offer in any given moment. Spontaneity indicates that we possess a significant level of consciousness as we trust that what comes our way is meant for us. We are not stuck in a repetitive comfort zone that limits infinite possibility. Spontaneous actions can be connected to miracles that we've been asking for in our lives. We may be responding to direct guidance and intuition: we receive a 'hit' and respond immediately. Go us!

Spontaneity often brings unparalleled joy. An example for me of spontaneous joy was one Saturday afternoon when my husband arrived home and said, 'There are snow clouds looming over the hills, let's pack a bag and head to Cradle Mountain for the night'.

A rush of excitement transported me back to that childlike sense of joy and wonder. The snow falling within half an hour of our leaving home added to the magic of spontaneity. It was like we were being rewarded for instantly changing direction and surrendering to a moment that was divinely inspired and created just for us.

A simple example of spontaneity was one Sunday night as I was heading to the kitchen to prepare dinner (not with much enthusiasm, I might add) and Pete said, 'Let's go for a spin up to Sheffield Chinese'. We were ready in ten minutes and winding our way up the country roads for an impromptu dinner. My kind of joy.

After any kind of spontaneity, it feels like I've had a total reboot. I always feel renewed enthusiasm for life. My creativity is ignited and a have a deep sense of peace that lasts for days. Routine is necessary at times, but spontaneity lights us up. Being spontaneous challenges us to be in the present moment, asking us to be willing to go in any direction in any moment. Spontaneity is true living and co-creating, with no resistance. Breaking routine and following the energy of spontaneity brings more flow and enthusiasm to my life, for days on end.

Affirmation

I readily receive the magical spontaneous opportunities that show up in my life with grace and enthusiasm.

> **My tip for your path to peace**
>
> If it feels light, say 'Yes' to what the universe has on offer, more than you say 'No'.

The essence

Spontaneity allows us to truly receive what the current moment is presenting. It is the space from which magic and miracles arise. Hear the call of your soul; it yearns for new experiences and expansion.

Stepping back

STEP BACK SO OTHERS CAN STEP UP.

One of the many gifts I've received (and a personal battle) in raising children is that I have learned over time to more fully surrender and let go. To do this, I have had to consciously work at stepping back in order to provide opportunities for my children to step up. This has occurred as a gradual release of responsibility, as I perceived that they were ready for me to do so. It has been an entirely different process for my daughter and my son. Our children are unique individuals and what works beautifully for one may not work with the other. An accompanying guidebook for both individuals would have been most handy, as all we have is our own parental intuition, combined with lots of trial and error and love to show us the way. Being kind and compassionate with our children and ourselves is key, as we do the best we can to navigate our way through some interesting and challenging scenarios.

We bring these beautiful little beings into the world and we nurture and protect them relentlessly. The challenge is to know when it is time to step back so they can learn to shine their own light, to connect more fully with their own inner guidance, and to learn to co-create their own unique lives with divine assistance. The temptation is to protect them, provide for them and sort everything out for them well beyond the time of letting go.

If we continue to control, fix and organise everything for our children, we hinder their ability to learn as quickly and to stand on their own feet, discovering what they are truly capable of achieving and creating in any moment. When we take on the role of micro-manager or helicopter parent, we are stepping into control. In this space we can never relax and trust in the flow and perfection of life. Our children can also inadvertently pick up on our fear that things may go wrong for them. They may not feel as valuable because (on some level) we are projecting a lack of trust in them as we are existing in a negative anticipatory state of what may happen next. Our worrying (although it can feel like at least we are doing something) sends toxic energy into the lives of our children and we certainly don't want that! We need to focus on the love that surrounds them and expect miracles. Guide them to be the best versions of themselves and at the same time allow them to take the reins in their journey through life. Empower them to know that they have the answers within—more than we do, as it is their journey.

> 'Parents are not for leaning upon;
> they are to make leaning unnecessary.'
> Dr Wayne Dyer

Affirmation

*I step back and allow my children
to shine in their own unique way.
I trust in their universal support team
and guidance.*

My tip for your path to peace

When your children are approaching their adult years, start the process of allowing them to make their own decisions and learn from their mistakes. The peace that awaits when they can manage their own fulfilling lives, and you trust that you've done your job, will be beautiful. Resist the urge to jump in and fix things; trust them and believe in the powerful beings that they can become.

The essence

We bring our children into the world so that they can connect with and shine their own light. We model all things conducive to leading a fulfilling, healthy life. When the timing is right, we step back and gradually set them free to connect with their own guidance system and step into their own power. Trust you will know when your children are ready.

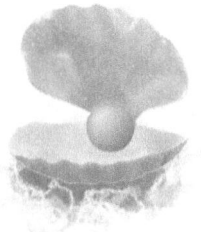

Stillness

STILLNESS ISN'T EMPTY,
IT CONTAINS POTENTIAL
AND ANSWERS.

Stillness places us in the now, that place where all potential and power begins. The potency of the now creates amazing futures, flows with possibilities and holds answers to all that we seek. When we are in stillness, all our energy is present within us; it is not filtered off into the past or wasted on escaping into a future that hasn't been created yet.

Sometimes life presents us with opportunities for stillness and reflection that we may not consciously have asked for. Opportunities may come through illness, or sudden changes in lifestyle that provide us with unexpected time or slowing down for looking within. Without the distraction of our day-to-day 'busyness', we get to pay attention and shine some light within.

Embrace challenges in life as they often force us (because we can no longer control our outside world) into a place of still, inner reflection for connecting with our power and wisdom. Adversity which forces us into the power of now brings out the best in us—it helps us unleash all the strength, light and greatness that we may have been hiding. We can become unstoppable.

> 'When you set your own light free,
> you become a veritable force of nature.'
>
> Danielle LaPorte

Find ways to bring stillness into your day to build momentum and flow. Moments taken for peace and calm help us to step into the space where creativity and inspiration abound. Creative pursuits assist to further focus and still our mind, bringing us into the now. Anything that captures our attention, and inspires or mesmerises us, provides access points to the now.

When we move out of stillness, problems and issues that exist (when we are in a frantic stressed state) are exacerbated. However, the flip side of this—which is retreating into stillness—can change the trajectory of our whole day. Suddenly intuition is reignited, connection with universal energy is re-established and problems can evolve into solutions.

Opportunities for stillness are everywhere, perhaps moments taken for a cup of tea, or sitting in nature, absorbing the sun while observing the bees at work. Stillness can be accessed through meditation and by focusing intently on what we are currently doing (without allowing the mind to wander to past events or projecting into the future). Jumping into the future is often a way to avoid the present moment when we have decided our 'present' is not enough. All we truly have is now, so we need to make it work for us. We have time. Now is the time.

Affirmation

*I am more powerful than my mind.
I use my mind with focus and intent
to build power in the present moment.*

My tip for your path to peace

Calm your mind through quieting experiences and watch your whole being, and events in your life calm. Stand still and perceive the power and peace that is within you. Radiate peace.

The essence

Value stillness more than you value 'busyness' and you will work less and achieve more, as all your power will be accessible to you, now. Stillness isn't empty, it flows with infinite wisdom and potential.

Stress

MAKE IT YOUR MISSION TO REDIRECT STRESSFUL REACTIONS TO PEACEFUL REACTIONS. THIS IS CRITICAL FOR WELLBEING.

Medical research often cites stress as a catalyst for ill health. Continued stress limits the ability of our body and mind to function at its best. Stress that is left unchecked can affect our thoughts, feelings, body and behaviour. It can create confusion and affect our ability to make decisions; our ability to choose wisely can also be compromised. Long-term stress can suppress the immune system, increase ageing, and contribute to depression, anxiety, digestive problems, skin problems and insomnia. It can also exacerbate pre-existing health problems because of the impact on wellbeing and the immune system.

> 'Science tells us that chronic long-term stress pushes the genetic buttons that create disease.'
>
> JOE DISPENZA

Stress also impacts those around us. If we are not functioning at our best, then our interactions can be less positive. Our relationships can suffer. Productivity and effectiveness in our workplace can also be hindered.

With stress we have choice, as we can ultimately choose the thoughts and corresponding emotions that come as a response to any given occurrence. We need to build the momentum and power of peace in our lives as our main priority. From here we have greater 'fuel' and ability to move through life's challenges with less impact on our health.

> 'Change stressful thoughts and change
> the way you process the world.'
> Dr Wayne Dyer

Excess 'busyness' can be an antagonist for stress, as we are not giving our bodies the chance to have a calm nervous system. This way of functioning can also come from an unwillingness to be in the present moment if we are constantly using 'busyness' to avoid looking at and experiencing what is. It can be another form of addiction as it helps us avoid dealing with unpleasant emotions, people or situations. It can be a way to disconnect. The choice to be excessively busy can take us out of flow as we are seeking control rather than surrender. This way of functioning can also be a sign of perfectionism that has taken over in an unhealthy and overwhelming way. Kindness to self and self-awareness are essential to release these types of unhealthy patterns.

Eckhart Tolle states that, 'if you are stressing or reacting you are in the grips of the ego, not in alignment'. It is our job, for the sake of our health, our sanity and our divine connection to dive into our toolkit and do what it takes to get back into alignment with our divine peaceful natures. This might be through prayer, reaching for feel-good emotions, positive affirmations (that you believe in as you are saying them), focusing on gratitude, nature experiences, meditation, yoga, grounding, breathing or reading inspirational literature. Each person's way back to alignment and away from stress will vary and change as spiritual awareness develops.

Affirmation

*Stressful reactions and thoughts are
not me and are not mine.
I acknowledge them as a means
of determining how I am functioning.
I take action to release stressful thinking and
reactions before they impact my wellbeing.*

My tip for your path to peace

Make meditation, positive thinking and relaxation experiences an essential part of your day. Watch for stressful reactions (like a hawk) and counteract them with something of equal strength to calm the nervous system and disengage the flight or fight mechanism.

The essence

Live from the space of seeking peace as your predominant intention. From here stressful moments have less impact. Manage your reactions, manage your stress and simultaneously change your health and way of living.

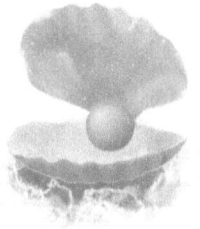

Success

**IT IS OUR BIRTHRIGHT.
ARE YOU READY TO STAKE
YOUR CLAIM?**

You are amazing! You've done the inner work; you've listened to your inner guidance and acted accordingly. Your prayers have been answered and then some. A dream has come true (it may even be a dream you didn't know you had), and standing before you is imminent success. What do you do from here? Do you panic and go to that familiar place of wanting to stay small, safe and hidden? The answer is maybe yes, initially—if you are anything like me and have had an addiction to hiding and to not being (too) seen or (too) heard. Or, do you 'rise up' even further, ready to show up and allow life to take you in new unexplored directions, deeply into that mystical unknown? When success first arrives, we can be in a challenging transition time. We aren't quite in the new space and vibration that success is calling us to step into being. For me, it feels like I am a balloon—one minute I'm expanding and feeling powerful and light and the next I'm slipping into my old pattern of contracting, of thinking it's more comfortable to stay small. We must say a resounding 'yes' to success and all that accompanies it, as the unknown contains even more of our creativity, enlightenment and bliss. We can relax into our peace as we know we are doing what we came here to do.

We need to be aware of what we are asking for when we show up as our true potential (radiating our strength, grace and power), as what we desire to call in can show up even more rapidly. There are no limits to the possibilities for expansion and creation.

Success is not an endpoint. It is a new beginning, a new chapter, an opportunity for more learning and growth. Success is the process of even more unfoldment of us as beings. Success calls us to let go, to surrender even more deeply into trust and to receive the magical flow and guidance that are available to us. We need to draw on all that we are and all that we came here to be. Perceiving even more fully just how amazing we are generates a powerful energy that invites in even more of our greatness.

Affirmation

*I relax into receiving the success that I have called in.
I am ready for this, I deserve this.
Success brings me unlimited rewards,
opportunities and bliss.*

My tip for your path to peace

Let go and just flow. When you've done the work and your faith is stronger than doubt, everything will be taken care of for you. Just be, allow and receive. Relax into the next phase of your journey.

The essence

Success can light us up and inspire us to rise up even more. It can allow us to step more deeply into the depths or our power, light and potential. Through our success we can access even more of the beautiful unknown world of unlimited possibility. Say yes to stepping through the new doorways that are opening just for you.

When a dream is delivered, it can be both amazing and scary. Avoid self-sabotage and commit to believing in yourself. Appreciate how much you deserve this, are ready for this and can handle this. You and your dreams are worth it.

Surrender

ALLOW THE UNIVERSE TO LEAD YOU, EVEN WHEN YOU DON'T KNOW WHERE IT'S TAKING YOU.

Surrender is following your intuition and doing what you can to pursue your dreams without needing to force, push, manipulate and control outcomes. Surrender is letting go of specific results, getting out of the way and opening to possibilities. It is being free of the need to know the 'how' associated with the way in which your desires manifest into reality. Having trust in divine timing is key. If something hasn't 'arrived' yet, it doesn't mean it's not coming. The universe is abundant with infinite possibilities. Faith in our divine connection and ability to co-create is paramount.

Through surrender we enter a state of flow. Life unfolds exactly as it is meant to, and we seem to be able to do less and attract more. Prayer and stillness help us to more effectively listen to our intuition and to then know how to act accordingly. Step back and allow what needs to go to leave, so you can create the space to allow what is meant to come (to do so) in divine timing. We know that what we ask for does not often show up as we've imagined. The universe often has a better plan for our highest good, one that best serves our journey and purpose in life. Embrace each step and lesson on the journey, as they have been perfectly designed for us.

Surrender fully to the present moment, as it is where we connect to the power within and to the guidance that is coming to us. Accept what is, and intuitively take steps from here, in the now.

Affirmation

*I surrender my dreams and plans
to the wisdom and care of the universe.
I trust it has a plan far greater than mine.
I connect with ease to the intuition
that guides me.*

My tip for your path to peace

Breathe, be still and surrender to the power within you and around you. Be at peace as everything is taken care of for you. Receive it all.

The essence

We transform our lives by practising the divine art of letting go. We follow our intuition, act as necessary and then surrender our dreams and plans to the care of the universe. We are limited by our imagination: the abundant, infinite universe is not.

Thoughts

WHAT WE SEND OUT VIA OUR THOUGHTS AND ACTIONS ATTRACTS 'LIKE' INTO OUR WORLD IN SOME WAY.

Be a person of precision and purpose as you use the power of your mind as a great instrument to positively impact your body and life. Life isn't randomly occurring; it is responding to us. Make each thought count as it travels like a beacon out into the world and brings back 'like' of some kind. Release negative and fearful thoughts before they gain momentum. Each cell in our bodies also responds to the content of our thoughts. Fill your body with thoughts of gratitude, health and wellbeing.

Tune into your thinking and remember that negative thoughts are ego-based and are designed to keep us limited. Don't allow them to gain momentum and power. Negative thinking can become addictive, as it often comes so easily to us, encouraging us to think we are doing something useful. The opposite is true, as we are fuelling negative emotions and a corresponding mindset. We need to make positive thinking our new normal, our natural default. Practise stopping any thoughts that involve self-criticism. Over time, self-criticism can keep us weak, undermine our self-worth, allow us to give away our power to others and make us vulnerable to manipulation. Be your own biggest supporter and use thoughts and take actions that uplift and inspire you.

Make it a practice to take your thinking away from the things that are not lighting you up. This helps release unhelpful and repetitive patterns. A very common form of negative thinking is worry. Worry often feels useful, as though we are attempting to change a situation. However, it puts negative energy around whoever or whatever is the focus of that type of thinking. Worry takes our energy away from proactive, life-enhancing thinking.

Affirmation

*I choose thoughts that light me up,
heal me and take me closer
to the person I choose to be.*

My tip for your path to peace

Peaceful emotions and attitudes come from peaceful thoughts. Make yours beautiful, for a calm mind and body. Choose thoughts consciously, selecting those that take you back to inner peace and contentment.

The essence

A peaceful, positive inner world is directly related to the stories we align with that eventually become our beliefs regarding ourselves and our experiences. The external world that we experience is a representation and reflection of repeated patterns of thinking over time. Change your thoughts, change your life.

Transformation

EVOLVING AND BLOOMING BEFORE YOUR EYES, AND INSPIRING OTHERS TO DO THE SAME.

Transformation is what those of us who came here to spread light (including you) endeavour to do throughout our lives, even if unacknowledged. It's the call to do and be something greater than we already are. We seek to make a difference: to serve, and to connect with universal magic, abundance, potential and wisdom. We are the learners of life. We observe ourselves and others, reflect and recalibrate to better ourselves. We grow and change in order to be the most powerful, conscious, aware versions of ourselves. We are not fans of an eternal comfort zone as we are always pushing forward to discover new frontiers within ourselves and in our understanding of how our world works. 'Transformers' know that the inner world is our most important focus and that our outer world is a representation of 'progress' as it reflects to us how we are functioning and what we are choosing.

Transformation occurs at an individual rate, slowly awakening during some stages of life and more rapidly at other times. Patience and compassion for self are key. We need to trust in our own journey and in the unique path that unfolds before us.

To truly transform we need a multifaceted approach. This includes a steady connection with our higher selves, tuning into our intuition, connecting with our spiritual team and embracing inspirational spiritual teachers and literature. Self-awareness is paramount. Wisdom is knowing what we do know, what we don't know and what we need to know, to move forward.

Self-care is an essential priority for successfully embracing transformation. Physical, emotional, mental and physical wellbeing are essential for bringing forth change and our best selves. We need to love and nurture ourselves to be most effective. Transformation is taxing work that requires bravery. As we let go of old patterns, we can feel very uncomfortable. To come out the other side we have to settle in and go through this process, often many times!

During any transitional stage, life can be confusing as we step into new ways of being and let go of what no longer serves us. Change is not easy and can feel very uncomfortable, as habits (including our beliefs and thought patterns) can be resistant to our attempts to transform. Letting go of the old to make way for the new can also bring up feelings of guilt or shame as we sometimes 'see' for the first time our limiting patterns—kindness and compassion for self is so needed here. Celebrate any new level of awareness, as we can't reach the point of letting go and transforming until we can truly see all that we are. During times of transition, certain things, situations and even people won't be as important to us as they used to be. We will often let go of what needs to go, in order to allow what needs to flow in and emerge. Our relationship with ourselves and the universe 'as a whole' will change during times of transition and transformation. We will come to see that being ourselves in all its glory really can impact life in a magnificent way.

All of human nature and potential exists within all of us—we are just at different stages of our healing and transformational journeys.

Each wound or fear that we transform moves us closer to freedom from our limiting shadow aspects and into our greatest potential. Strong boundaries, protecting our energies, staying peaceful and accessing our power and wisdom assist us to successfully navigate the many challenges that serve as our teachers. We are on the pathway for transforming into our best 'butterfly' ever!

Affirmation

*Every day is an opportunity to transform
that which no longer serves me into
that which empowers me and lights me up.
I am transformazing!*

My tip for your path to peace

Be at peace with what you require for growth and change. It won't be the same as it is for anyone else. Embrace your journey and uniqueness with calm assurance that all is as it's meant to be.

The essence

Our transformational time frame and journey are unique to us. Transformation is what our souls call for us to do. As we shine our light and awaken, so too will those around us, as they can't help but respond to our presence, our example and the inspirational beings that we've become.

You are a gift to this world. The butterfly has at last emerged from her cocoon in ways beyond what she could have imagined. The universe thanks her for her commitment and rewards her in ways that are just for her.

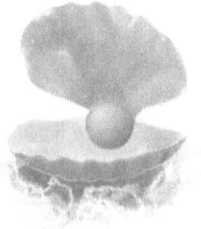

Travel

'WHERE TO NEXT FOR INSPIRATION?'

Travel is pure nourishment for the mind and spirit as we discover and appreciate places of beauty and interest. The very act of packing a bag and leaving for a new destination implies moving forward into uncharted territories. Travel tricks us into believing we are creating a new life as we temporarily leave our current conditions behind. It creates a unique space for creativity and inspiration. Travel forces us into the power of the present moment as our eyes and senses take in new sights and experiences. Experiences that inspire and excite keep us in creative mode—which is truly living. For me, travel changes my thinking patterns, and as I welcome in new thoughts, aspects of my life begin to change.

A new view, a change of scenery and a deviation from routine brings possibility for inspiration and new thinking. Changes in thinking contribute to new life as conditioned patterns which can make us feel like each day is playing on repeat are unblocked. Doing something or seeing something for the first time or even from a new perspective provides sparks of inspiration and joy for our spirit, which is a beautiful way to live.

Travel can help us transform aspects of ourselves and our lives into something more amazing as we step further into the possibility of a surprise-filled, unknown future.

Travel breaks us free of the mundane and allows our wings to unfurl. We access the wings we were born with, and fly. Just planning a trip is adventure itself, as we dream, create, research, imagine and learn.

Travel changes us on a deep level as our hearts and minds open to new ideas, cultures, values and ways of living and being. We are challenged to see things from different perspectives. We experience 'surprises' that provoke our thinking and cause us to look at things in new ways.

Experiencing things for the first time lights up our inner child and reminds us to bring a sense of adventure and newness into our lives. Moving outside our comfort zone into unknown places and situations stretches us to grow and maintain a sense of curiosity, awe and wonder. There are endless sights, people, cities and experiences, just waiting for us to discover and fall in love with— to enrich our lives.

Travel brings gratitude for the lives we have temporarily left behind as we miss family, friends, homes, familiar environments and careers. Travel turns us into storytellers. We develop closer connections with others as we share what we've seen and where we've been. Travel is a universal connector as more and more people make travel a vital part of their living.

Affirmation

*I am willing to travel
out of my comfort zone to
discover new destinations,
beauty and adventure.*

My tip for your path to peace

Pack a bag and leave for a new destination as often as you can, even if it's only a skip and a jump from your home. Peace arises when leaving behind the routine pressures of our daily lives.

The essence

Travel brings fresh energy and inspiration to our lives and we open to new ways of seeing, feeling and being.

Trusting your future

YOUR FUTURE EXISTS BEYOND YOUR IMAGINATION—THE UNIVERSE HAS EVEN GRANDER PLANS FOR YOUR LIFE.

Sometimes we think we'd like to know the future, but do we really? Allow your life and destiny to unfold as a beautiful story that is yet to be written.

Taking care of today and placing all of our energy here takes care of the future. Everything we build in the moment works for us in creating our future. Get free of repeating old patterns and living in the past. From the present moment we can create a future that isn't a conditioned replica of the past.

'Knowing' your future can act as a self-fulfilling prophecy. Even when future events can be predicted, change in trajectory can occur in a heartbeat if you step up or change your outlook in any way. It is a free-will universe and life is your adventure to create. Psychic predictions may be accurate one day and not the next: potential accuracy depends on the choices you make and is also determined by the current 'energies' that are being connected with during the reading. Clairvoyants decode messages received through their own senses (and lens), so it's all open to interpretation. Claim your own power by co-creating your own dreams and visions without needing validation or reassurance. You have all the answers within you. Avoid going to fear, negativity or doubt. It's too easy and too detrimental to go there.

What would you create and what would your life look like if you had faith that you were always being guided?

Decide that where you are is the perfect place to be. Finding the good wherever you are brings forth more. Trust and joy are great catalysts for attracting more of what we require and desire.

Affirmation

The universe is always on my side, supporting, creating and taking care of all that is required for me to live my purpose and create an expansive life.

My tip for your path to peace

Follow what lights you up to find peace. Peace exists when we are not resisting what is in front of us. If it lights our fire, there is less chance of experiencing the heavy energy of resistance. Trust that when you are on the path of joy you are drawing to you exactly what your life requires to move forward, and there is peace in that. You and universe have already taken care of your future. Be at peace with that.

The essence

We need to keep trusting and having unwavering faith in ourselves and in what the universe is co-creating with us. This allows us to live a life that is on purpose, uniquely designed for us and is in service to our highest good.

Understanding

**WE ARE ALL HERE TOGETHER …
JUST ON DIFFERENT PARTS OF
THE JOURNEY.**

Understanding creates peace as we are less likely to go to judgement or react from an ego perspective to what we are encountering with another. From a place of understanding, we see others as a mirror for what is going on within us rather than as us being unconnected, unrelatable and separate. When understanding is in play, we continually contribute to growth and healing for each other as our perceptions involve greater awareness and truth. We are willing to perceive our own limitations and greatness, when we allow others to be 'mirrors' for how we are currently functioning and responding to life.

Seeing through the eyes of someone else, or being able to stand in their shoes, gives to them in immeasurable ways, as compassion heals. Healing flows when we are present with a friend in need. Acknowledgement of another's experience, combined with respect, validates what someone is encountering. The elevated state of combining the power of 'present' and compassionate individuals creates the space for each to access their own healing.

It is important that understanding comes from a place of empathy rather than sympathy. Empathy is empowering, as it encourages one to look within to find guidance and direction. Being empathetic encourages the recipient (through our presence, energy and responses to their needs) to change their own problems to solutions, by helping to create the space for them to connect with their own inner wisdom. Sympathy often comes from a place of pity and superiority, and doesn't encourage personal growth and connection. Being sympathetic can imply that we hold all the answers and can allow the recipient's possible 'pity party' to be fuelled, and that's the opposite of being helpful and effective harbingers of change.

If understanding is our priority, our relationships will be more positive, peaceful and based on love. Our partnerships will be based on equality and mutual respect, with a healthy dose of compassion mixed in. Imagine how this could change our friendships, family, village, town, city, country and world.

Affirmation

*I easily put judgement aside,
embrace my understanding nature,
and connect deeply with others
in ways that uplift us both.*

My tip for your path to peace

After your initial judgement of another or a situation, stop, breathe and ask: 'What else could I truly perceive that I've been unwilling or unable to see?' Understanding and compassion for self and others promotes peace.

The essence

Choose to see the light in another person as a basis for developing understanding. See any shadow aspects that you may perceive in others as parts of you that you haven't yet acknowledged or fully healed. Embrace the healing power of awareness, understanding and compassion.

Universal guidance

LISTEN AND CO-CREATE YOUR LIFE
TO THRIVE RATHER THAN SURVIVE.

How did we get so lucky to be able to access a wisdom beyond our wildest dreams? We are spiritual beings fortunate enough to be experiencing life on earth. We came to earth with amazing dreams and intentions. Unfortunately it is all too easy to get derailed or distracted from our purpose and mission. Our universal team of angels, guides and masters is in place ready to guide and nudge us in the right direction whenever we require it; we just need to ask.

We have the ability to tune into universal guidance with greater ease—we just need to align our frequency with our divine source. To stay in alignment, we can work on maintaining elevated emotions to raise our vibration and do what is required to calm our minds. When we quiet the ego part of our minds and stay in the present moment, we can hear the whispers of the universe that are stirring just for us. Any form of quieting activity, whether it's a cup of tea in our garden while listening to the birds, feeling the breeze on our skin, or indulging in some meditation, can help us to access universal guidance and to co-create our lives with flow rather than force.

Moving from a place of needing to control and coordinate every aspect of our lives into a place of trust and surrender delivers unimaginable and unexpected peace. From this space we can receive beyond what we could conjure, relishing in unexpected and amazing twists and turns that lead us forward in life. To remove ourselves from the limited 'being in control merry-go-round,' we need to ask for universal guidance and concurrently release being vested in set outcomes. We then create the space to receive information coming through in the form of intuitive hits, signs, symbols, conversations, music and in magical ways unique to each person. The universe delivers what we are willing to receive, what we can handle, and what is for our highest good.

Affirmation

I easily clear my mind to access universal wisdom for co-creating my phenomenal life.

My tip for your path to peace

Make it a daily practice to breathe, quiet the mind and receive universal guidance to allow life to unfold with flow and ease. Co-creating our lives is peaceful and fulfilling, as we are never alone in our endeavours.

The essence

Accessing universal guidance means that we can trust that we are never alone in facing the myriad of beautiful challenges life gives us and that the blessings and bounty in life are available for us.

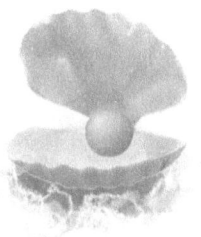

Unrequited love

LET GO AND ALLOW THE LOVE
MEANT FOR YOU TO COME
YOUR WAY.

Unrequited love, for those who experience it, seems like a rite of passage that is essential to go through. When we emerge from the other side of this somewhat tumultuous, obsessive, self-worth-challenging and seemingly so significant experience, we finally perceive that rejection really is a form of protection. The aftermath for me has always been a sense of relief. Thank goodness that didn't come to fruition! Or if it had happened, I wouldn't have met ⎯⎯ or been ⎯⎯ or done ⎯⎯.

Unrequited love has often felt like a type of holding pattern keeping me expertly occupied until I have been truly ready to receive the individuals who have been meant for me to arrive at various times in life. This kind of love was the most wonderful distraction, providing great practice to store up loads of love in readiness for when the person meant for me showed up. Moving through unrequited love into the sense of relief (on the other side) has always created trust—deeply knowing that the universe really does have my back and has a far greater plan for me than I could have conjured.

Unrequited 'loves' can still hold a place in our hearts for the lessons in love they've given us. You may be surprised if you ever run into any of these old flames just how much the dimmer switch has been turned down and how free and powerful you feel! There may even be a touch of, 'What was I thinking?' It was what it was: lessons learned, growth instigated—what a gift!

Affirmation

I am deserving of that person who is meant just for me, and I am ready to receive this great love.

My tip for your path to peace

Thank all your 'unrequited loves' energetically for all the time they allowed you to both feel love and also to hold that space in readiness for the one meant for you.

The essence

Embrace love in all its diverse forms. Each love that is lost moves us one step closer to the love meant especially for us.

Variety and versatility

YES, YOU REALLY CAN HAVE AND BE IT ALL.

Variety is about experiencing difference and diversity with the absence of uniformity or monotony. Versatility implies that we can live life on life's terms, adapting to and connecting with what is presented to us. Being flexible, versatile and open to co-creation throughout all our days leads to an inspired, adventurous, big life. Variety and versatility keep us alert and promote the creation of new neural pathways in the brain, as there is less chance of familiar patterns conditioning our minds over and over in the same way, in effect re-creating the past instead of creating new futures.

Variety and versatility assist us to reconnect to our childlike sense of wonder and awe, as they encourage our presence and belief in the magnificence of life. Surprises and new directions brighten our existence, as they are unexpected gifts that raise our vibration through the sheer joy they create. Variety entertains us and adds life to all our connections and relationships. Being versatile reduces our chances of being reactionary or stressed, as we are more able to adapt, adjust and go with the flow. It is a great practice for us to pause regularly for a personal reset and review, to identify where some variety and versatility could be added to enrich our lives.

What could you see differently or from a new perspective today?

Where could you go? Who could you meet?

What story could you tell yourself about you (or someone else) that is different from yesterday's story?

What new possibilities could you open to today?

Become a living 'question', always asking the universe for more ways to experience variety and versatility. If we do the same things over and over, there is a fair chance that our patterns of behaviour and life experiences won't deviate much, or change. Monotony is the antithesis of variety and versatility.

To incorporate the wonderful states of variety and versatility, we can start simply. Even if it's just to drive a different way to work, eat at a different spot, reinvent our dress style, or change our exercise or after-work routine, it's all showing the universe that we are open to newness and variety. We become more versatile and in turn draw more variety into our lives, as we more readily receive and embrace what our amazing universe can offer.

Affirmation

*I thrive on variety; it makes me feel alive.
I am excited by the possibilities and opportunities available in each new day.
Versatility allows me to flow with grace and peace as I effortlessly navigate new life.*

My tip for your path to peace

By embracing what life presents, we are free of any resistance to what is. This helps us to remain centred, calm and connected to our inner peace.

The essence

We need to be versatile in order to fully embrace variety: the spice of life and the zest for life. Variety and versatility breathe new life into our bodies, hearts and minds.

Visibility

SHINE YOUR LIGHT SO OTHERS CAN FIND YOU.

For some reason many of us adopt the mantra of 'be unseen and unheard'. For me, I gained comfort from choosing to be the quiet achiever in the background, being the girl who didn't draw too much attention to herself. From this space, no-one bothered me or had expectations or demands that I wasn't ready to fulfil. The problem with attempting invisibility was that I was also inadvertently hiding from myself and hiding from my own potential for greatness. I had developed a decades-long addiction to hiding and it was time to be free!

Many of us appear to be afraid of our own greatness because if we embrace it, we might have to show up as our most brilliant, creative and expansive selves. With that comes shining our light and stepping up in ways we've previously decided are highly uncomfortable and definitely not for us. Unfortunately, with this, we often deprive ourselves of the true, big life and the destiny that is calling us forward.

We need to surrender our resistance to shining bright. The world needs the contribution we can make through consistently putting the best, most amazing version of ourselves forward. Stepping up and into our potential is what creates miracles as the ripple effect on others, situations and events is incomparable and causes us to thrive. Showing up as our most expansive, brightest self touches others and gives them 'permission' and the inspiration to do the same. When we become visible and are willing to reveal all our greatness, talents and abilities, we get to discover how wonderful we are, and others get to see it too. Our willingness to be seen, along with perceiving ourselves as amazing, raises our vibration and fuels our motivation to create and be more. This in turn draws amazing opportunities and people into our lives. From this space, everybody will want to work with us and connect with us. We will be true leaders, forging a pathway for others to discover and embrace their own greatness.

Avoid the trap of making yourself smaller, or less than, or less visible, in order to make others people feel more secure around you. The world needs you to be expansive and bright in order to effectively serve, lead and create change.

Affirmation

I claim my power, talents and abilities and step into being the magnificence I truly am.

My tip for your path to peace

Adopt the stance of having no resistance to what is or to what is coming for you in terms of your potential visibility. Stepping into your greatness will bring peace as you surrender and show up—without a fight. Procrastination and resistance are the antithesis of peace.

The essence

Staying hidden makes us feel safe and comfortable, but limits us (and the contribution we are here to make) as our talents and abilities can lie dormant or completely obscured from us and others. When choosing invisibility, we don't get to enjoy the full capacity of our light and neither does anyone else.

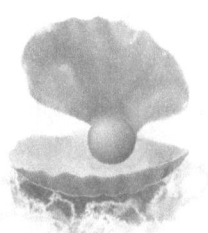

Vulnerability

BRAVERY AND SELF-KNOWLEDGE ARE
FOUND ON THE OTHER SIDE
OF VULNERABILITY.

Vulnerability is true strength. Strong people are prepared to seek support and look within to see the whole truth of themselves. Vulnerability allows us to surrender. We momentarily give up control when we know it is okay to let go. Being vulnerable sets us free to heal, change and unleash all our amazingness, as there is nothing holding back our ability to look within and to explore changing what limits us. Be courageous and work towards identifying the shadow aspects and reactive triggers that may be limiting you. Allow self-awareness through vulnerability to be yours.

Vulnerability helps us to shine, as it reveals our authentic, most powerful, most honest self. Honouring the truth about ourselves sets us free to go in new directions. We can create ourselves anew, as we are not in the dark about ourselves: we can be our own open book for learning, healing, growing and evolving. If we can't show vulnerability, we tend to put forward the dimmed-down version that 'fits in' with those around us. Attempting to be a 'chameleon of strength' in all situations is draining, stressful and not conducive to optimal wellbeing. We leak a lot of energy when attempting to keep the facade of strength and invulnerability in place.

Relationships and connections are enhanced through vulnerability. As we lower our guard and show more of the real us, those around us feel safe and trust us, as we are not creating false images or wearing any masks. We share, they share: vulnerability creates beautiful reciprocal, balanced connections. The world needs authentic individuals who are willing to be vulnerable enough to be truly seen and to unleash their full potential. When revealing our vulnerability, we encourage others to honour themselves enough to go where we've gone to embrace discovery of self and ensuing greatness.

Affirmation

*I acknowledge how strong
I truly am by consistently identifying
what I need to heal and release.
I look within and seek assistance
(as needed) for stepping into
being the best version of me.*

My tip for your path to peace

Being comfortable enough and worthy enough to reveal how you feel and who you are, allows a sense of peace to prevail. In this space we are trusting rather than working against ourselves. Practise vulnerability at first with those you trust and who have your best interests at heart. Peace comes from supporting ourselves and in seeking all that we need to relax into our inner calm and contentment.

The essence

Be willing to be everything you are. You will come to know yourself more deeply as you bravely identify what you need in order to heal and grow. Lowering your guard and embracing vulnerability will allow those around you to enjoy you, to respect you and to trust in the authentic you.

Work

AN EXTENSION OF OUR LIVING.

Love your work and love your life. If we work from a place of joy, all those around us feel it. Appreciation and gratitude for our efforts will come our way and we will feel good about ourselves. We will feel successful as we are contributing in a way that serves others and makes a difference. Productive and valuable work adds meaning to our days. We need our lives to feel purposeful and to be meaningful.

Our work needs to be a part of our conscious living. Inspired work leads to an inspired, creative, expansive and fulfilling life. A big life in all its glory, with both challenges and triumphs, is possible if we enjoy our work. All jobs, no matter what they entail, that are performed with care and lightness of being impact others. Individuals who approach work in this way are of great value as they assist in the healing of those around them with the light and energy they spread.

If your current work is unfulfilling, strive to build positive energy (to attract in new possibilities) by finding joy and being grateful for what is, whenever possible. Remember the universe delivers more of what we focus on, so if we focus on how unhappy we are at work then it is likely that we will get more of the same. Follow what lights you up and create joy in every day in some way, no matter how seemingly small, to attract more of what you are seeking. The trick is to find gratitude and ways of enjoying whatever work we are doing, even if the job is not something we want to be doing in the long term. Maybe revamp your office, find ways to enjoy more connection and laughter with colleagues, or organise more workplace social events. Do whatever it takes to build positive energy around the work that you do, to increase the likelihood of drawing new possibilities into your world.

Always do your best in all that you do. We create meaningful change, synchronicities and miraculous opportunities from a space of appreciation, peace and contentment. Fight the urge to be a complainer in the job you currently have, as there is often no space for miracles from there, just more to complain about. Value your day job while you are working on creating the career you truly desire. For whatever reason, we have the work that we attracted in. Do the time; receive the lessons; embrace the experiences you need for personal growth and healing (and the pay cheque) and move on when appropriate.

Affirmation

I find a sense of achievement in all that I do, and I know that life is always working to bring me more.

> **My tip for your path to peace**
>
> Offer no resistance to what is, just appreciation. At the same time, cultivate exquisite dreams for your future phenomenal career. There is peace in this space.

The essence

Our work should be a beautiful extension of our life. It is our way of contributing to our life and that of others. Enjoy and appreciate the fruits of your labour to bring forth more fruit.

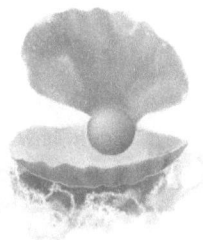

Worry

LET IT GO AND CREATE MORE
SPACE FOR YOU.

There is a great saying, 'Worrying is like walking around with an umbrella waiting for it to rain'. Whoever wrote this nailed what worry feels like for me. It reminds me of the futility of worry, along with the wasted energy, emotions and thinking associated with worry. Worrying can make us feel like at least we are doing 'something' when confronted with challenging situations. Unfortunately, the opposite is true. Worrying doesn't change or improve anything. It hinders our ability to use our thoughts and energy productively for creating miracles. Worrying about those we love can send negative, toxic energy in their direction. We need to watch our thoughts so that worrying does not become our mind's default system. If we keep worrying about the same things, we get the same things to worry about. Our thoughts create our lives; we do not want to be creating our lives on an autopilot of worry.

I asked a client (who was having many a sleepless night, worrying about her son) to practise in bed each night picturing all the wonderful attributes she would like to see develop within him, and also the types of things she'd like to see happening in his life. Almost immediately her stress levels improved, and his behaviour started to change. He stopped smoking and drinking, started to communicate with her for the first time about the suffering he was experiencing, and reached out for help. The changes in the whole family dynamic as a result were miraculous. An extremely turbulent household managed to find a greater degree of peace.

A strategy that has always worked for me is to put my latest worry in a 'compartment' for a time so that I can deal effectively with the issue behind the worry. If it is something that is beyond my control to fix or change, then I surrender it to the care of the universe. By placing it in a compartment, I don't allow thoughts and emotions to infiltrate and taint other current situations in my life.

Excessive worry (that becomes uncomfortable and anxiety-inducing) can be the final trigger and gift that can force us to let go of control. From here we often surrender to a higher power and eventually trust that the universe always does have our back, if we will allow it.

Affirmation

I focus on the light and love that surrounds me and I anticipate miracles.

My tip for your path to peace

Reprogram worrying thoughts into positive alternatives and watch greater peace transcend.

The essence

Worrying indicates that we have lost trust in the universe. We are anticipating the worst rather than trusting that there is divine order to our lives. Trust that everything happens for our highest good. Surrender even the slightest concerns to the universe and expect miracles.

X-rated or A-rated

COME OUT OF JUDGEMENT AND SET YOURSELF FREE.

Being free of judgement and not having to decide whether someone or something is 'A-rated or X-rated' in every moment of every day is true liberation, as we are in allowance of what is currently presenting in life, without ego reactions or unhelpful mind commentary. Imagine the peace that would be in our hearts, minds and lives if we were able to be free of judgement of ourselves and others. The ripple effects, not only in our lives but also in our family, town and country, would be phenomenal.

All that we see and experience in life is judged or not judged through our own lens. Our 'lens' is shaped by all the experiences enjoyed or endured throughout life, and the behaviours, ideas and attitudes we've had modelled by those around us. What one person might consider R-rated or totally off limits could be the norm for another. Often what we judge is a mirror reflecting our own points of view both known to us and unknown. We often judge in others what we refuse to acknowledge within ourselves. Judgement can be a way we define ourselves in comparison or 'against' others. We judge others and are inadvertently deciding 'we are not that.' More than likely the opposite is true and there is a lesson, an insight within our judgement, if we are aware enough to perceive it.

These days, each time I judge someone I get a little excited. This is because I know I'm on the brink of learning more about myself and getting free of more limitation, and creating more conscious awareness. Take note of what you judge in others, or a trait that you react to as a way of discovering (and then shining light on) your own disowned or shadow aspects. Our judgement of others is a protective (numbing) mechanism that we use so as not to have to face our own wounded self. Judgement is a distraction from looking at what is truly going on within us.

Judgement is sometimes triggered when we perceive we have lost control of our current conditions or environment. Blaming situations or people for our discontent can be a natural response allowing us to avoid what is occurring at an inner level for us. Being out of control can also trigger old wounds and addictive patterns. Judgement and its temporary numbing tendency (for our own pain) can be very addictive. Judgement always cuts us off from our own wisdom and peace. We need to shine awareness on the wounds that are underneath our judgement whenever we can, and at the same time do what we can to move back into alignment with our higher self, the part of us that is always at peace.

As I have evolved, I have witnessed my own versions of judgement and have acknowledged what a destructive force it has truly been. For years, it was such a natural response—everything I did or said was judged. My self-judgement was way harsher than anything I could come up with for others. I was my own personal judge, jury and gaoler, but would generally be okay allowing others to be whatever they wanted to be. Becoming aware of judgement (as the unkind and untrue ego voice in my head) was the start of getting free. We can't heal what we can't see or acknowledge within ourselves.

I have also learned on my healing journey that judging others was the way I was keeping myself safe—or that is how my ego was convincing me that what I was doing was justified. My judgements of others would show up mostly if I perceived someone to be mean, unkind or behaving or doing something that I didn't approve of, as a way for me to separate and withdraw from them. It was connected to not trusting myself, or the flow of life. Judgement had become my way of not letting anyone get too close, if I had 'decided' (for whatever reason) they shouldn't be getting too close. On some strange level, this approach felt like I was protecting myself, but all it was doing was blocking connection and my own potential. We can't have what we are unwilling to receive—and that was apparently a whole lot!

Judgement is destructive for our bodies and lives, as we are often functioning from a stress response and from low fear-based vibes. Judgement is the opposite of being in a state of gratitude and allowance, and is the antithesis of love. Whenever we direct judgement at another it always flows back negatively into our own space and lives; such is the nature of karma.

There is another side of judgement: when you are the recipient of judgement from others. Many people in our lives can have strong points of view on whether what we are doing or choosing is A-rated or X-rated. Remember to never take judgement personally, as it is never about you; it's a reflection of how another is responding to and reacting to life and what is going on within them. What someone is judging in you is just a representation of what they are refusing to see in themselves. Judgement is never what it appears to be; there is always something more under the surface. Avoid validating the negativity of others by taking on their judgements of you, as we can lock this low energy into our minds and bodies, and it can seriously undermine our self-worth. Their 'experience' is their experience and does not have to impact us. They will change if they choose to change; it's not up to us to do the work for another. Learning to change our own responses is what sets us free.

Judgement blocks our flow and keeps us further from our dreams. Change the momentum of judgement by doing whatever is possible to raise your vibration. Sometimes it can be as simple as redirecting our thinking back to gratitude and appreciation, or doing something for someone else. Delivering kindness always helps to raise our vibration and make us feel better about ourselves. Beautiful self-worth is an antidote for judgement against self and others. The more you love yourself and your life, the less programs of judgement will be able to take root. To further protect your self-worth, avoid judging yourself for judging! Just witness your judgements and compassionately seek to do better next time. We need to celebrate how amazing we are each time we witness our judgements. Every time we bring awareness to the program, we are one step closer to freedom.

Judgement is the primary way that we cut ourselves off from our greatness and potential. Judging ourselves and others keeps us stuck in a limited universe, away from our life of infinite possibilities. The more we rise up and stand in our light, the less power we allow the ego in leading us down the path of judgement.

Affirmation

Each day I work to identify my patterns of judgement. I choose to be free from judgement so I can feel good. I am in total allowance of what life presents.

My tip for your path to peace

Before making a judgement, breathe and ask to look through eyes of love rather than through seemingly preprogrammed habitual and conditioned responses. The less reactive we are, the more we access our peaceful parasympathetic nervous system. Freedom from negative reactions is a recipe for a more peaceful existence. Without judgement we are free to receive all that is, from a place of surrender and flow. We can live in peace through acceptance.

The essence

Every person perceives people, situations and events in a different way depending on their own reference points and life experiences. Be in a place of accepting all the blessed variety that exists on planet Earth. This will allow greater freedom from negative, harmful reactions. These responses interfere with our ability to look within as the means to change what is standing in the way of our peaceful existence.

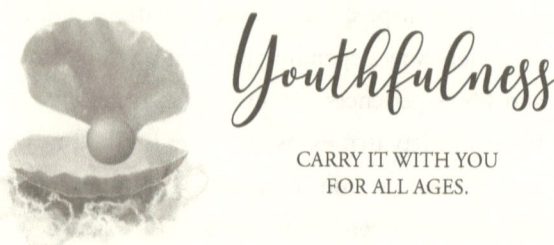

Youthfulness

CARRY IT WITH YOU
FOR ALL AGES.

Youthfulness is to a large degree a point of view. It isn't as determined by age in numbers as we might think it is. Our bodies respond to our thoughts—we can focus on messages that convince our bodies that they are vibrant, healthy and youthful. Taking care of ourselves physically, emotionally, mentally and spiritually maintains a positive and therefore youthful approach to life. Our inner space and all aspects of how we approach our wellbeing significantly determine how we 'age'.

Keeping a childlike sense of fun, wonder, inspiration and awe assists us to create the light within to defy aging. Qualities such as kindness, compassion and self-worth create a sense of love and peace within the heart and help maintain our youthful, efficient functioning. Kindness, compassion and gratitude are essential ingredients for the inner light that then becomes an outward youthful glow.

How we perceive ourselves affects our outward appearance; we need to strive to enhance our self-worth. If our self-worth is high, we will value ourselves enough to indulge in the self-care we require. We will also function from a positive space, focusing on our wellness, rather than illness, and our bodies will respond in kind. As like is magnetically attracted to like, we will draw in more positivity and joy, which are the true elixirs of youth. We will radiate an aura of beauty and youthfulness, which is a direct representation of how we feel within.

Get free of definitions of what should or shouldn't be done, worn or said at specific ages. Avoid buying into a society-created age reality. Create your own version of what age looks like and feels like. Assign your own meaning to what it means to be blessed enough to live a long time in numbers. What if advanced years on earth could mean increased wisdom, self-worth, inner and outer beauty, inner peace and the vitality of youth?

Affirmation

My body and life work all day, every day to rejuvenate and restore my youthfulness and vitality.

My tip for your path to peace

Embrace with grace, gratitude and no resistance your healthiest happiest life, to bring a sense of peace to whatever 'age' you are.

The essence

Our points of view around ageing can create our reality. Take care of yourself daily (spiritually, mentally, emotionally and physically) to slow and even reverse the ageing process.

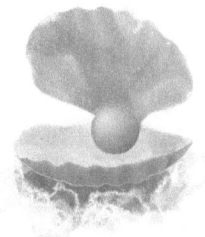

Zaniness

SUPERCHARGE YOUR LIFE WITH FIRE IN YOUR SPIRIT AND AMUSEMENT IN YOUR HEART.

'Zany' can be defined as 'unconventionally amusing'. Zaniness allows us to spread light and joy. It can awaken those who may be trapped in limitation, or held back by the security of conventionality. Modelling zaniness can assist those who feel they need to dim themselves in order to fit in, to step into embracing more of their greatness. Zaniness brings an energy of light and a renewed enthusiasm for life.

Sometimes we become so accustomed to playing certain roles in our lives that we forget to 'play' with a zaniness that can be contagious, spreading joy and childlike fun. We need to drop our masks and embrace silliness and humour in situations where we have decided we shouldn't—just for a change. Watch how some zaniness makes others light up and gives them an excuse to drop their own masks and roles.

Being zany can create a renewed sense of freedom and possibility. Throughout our lives, we take on many roles, often originating in childhood. It might be the role of the peacemaker, the adviser, the antagonist, the nurturer, the entertainer, the organiser and so on. Unfortunately, these roles can follow us through life and become so ingrained that we forget to branch out and try new roles that might suit our current life situation and level of consciousness. Defined roles can be a source of limitation and stress. Imagine the peace we could have in life if we created ourselves day to day, rather than having to adhere to defined roles. Let the zaniness spread; it may be just the ingredient needed to create yourself anew. Out of zaniness comes new ways of being, inspiration and creativity.

Affirmation

I give myself permission to discover all that I am by embracing and allowing my zany uniqueness to show up whenever it wishes to express itself.

My tip for your path to peace

Be who you are, no matter how different and unorthodox you may be. This will give you a peaceful sigh of 'being yourself' relief, and will give others permission to respond in like. Peaceful interactions will result as everyone is free to be who they are.

The essence

Move into experimenting with new ways of being that are aligned with who you truly are. Be different with a dash of zaniness to break norms and allow others to step up and be the difference they can be.

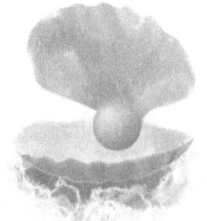

Zzz... sleep

HEAL AND REPLENISH AND START
EACH DAY ANEW.

OH, MY BED! HOW DO I LOVE THEE!
LET ME COUNT THE WAYS.

Sleep is self-care. It is the time when we most effectively process and release whatever has occurred during the day. Sleep is our renewal and repair time, physically, mentally, spiritually and emotionally. Sleep reduces stress hormones and assists our immune system to better serve us. Each new day is a new beginning, particularly if we are replenished through sleep.

Our creativity and memory are enhanced through sleep. Very often upon waking, flashes of insight come through. Clear thinking is more likely after we've 'slept on it'. Often if we go to sleep with a question on our mind, the answer will be evident upon waking. Setting intentions before we sleep is a powerful practice, for example, 'tonight I will remember my dreams'.

During sleep we connect with the heavenly realms. The universe whispers to us as we receive guidance and inspiration. Our dreams are healing. Dreams that are beautiful and disturbing are equally healing. Both help us to process emotions we have been unable to release during our waking hours.

Sleep is healing as our bodies and minds can do what they do best: restoring us on all levels. Don't ever underestimate the healing power of sleep; miracles occur physically, emotionally, mentally and spiritually while we slumber away. Don't stress if you have wakeful nights. Just resting is still healing. Work out what you can do to resettle if you're having trouble sleeping. Thinking positive, gratitude and heart-warming thoughts along with deep breathing is key for me. A simple mantra like 'all is well' or 'love and peace surround me' helps to still reckless thoughts—and I'm drifting off again before I know it.

Our bedrooms should be sanctuaries. Fill them with soft furnishings and subtle lighting. Make your bedroom the place where you let the day slip away and peace can prevail. Well before bedtime, imagine the feeling of snuggling in, as it is heavenly nurturing. Set the mood. Be warm and cosy.

Have a bedtime ritual or two as you prepare yourself for a restful night ahead. I always enjoy a shower or bath and imagine washing off the day. It signals to my body and mind that it's nearly time for sleep. After some pampering, I hop into bed and choose my favourite essential oil to rub on my feet. There is always lots of choice on my nightstand, my own little apothecary centre. A collection of beautiful crystals also adorns my bedside table. Next, it's reaching for my latest novel and usually having a quick 'book club chat' with hubby, who's equally thrilled to be in our cocoon. I find reading a sure-fire way to wind down and access joy and peace prior to sleep. Next, it's cuddles and 'I love you' and I'm ready for a night of exciting adventure in dreamland. I also like a tiny slither of light and at least some fresh air flowing into the room. Before sleep, I recap the day, focusing particularly on moments of gratitude. I then allow the day to become the past, knowing deeply that tomorrow is a new day.

Work out if there are any particular 'triggers' that keep you awake or contribute to nights of disturbed sleep. My triggers are caffeine consumed at any point in the day, alcohol, foods with too many additives, screen time, and watching intense movies prior to sleep. Most importantly, processing and releasing any negative emotions or reactions from the day (prior to bed) promotes sleep. I want my bedtime sanctuary to be free of anything negative before I enter. We need to make the demand on ourselves that we 'clear' the day before bed, and it will become a life-changing habit.

Affirmation

I am a brilliant sleeper.
I drift off with ease and enjoy a dream-filled tranquil sleep.
I awake feeling rested and positive about the day to come.

My tip for your path to peace

Let go of the day and focus only on peaceful thoughts. Fill your mind with positive thoughts of gratitude, love and appreciation to encourage drifting off into a peaceful, blissful sleep.

The essence

Sleep is a form of self-care. It is essential for healing and moving through life with vitality and positivity. Prioritise the development of healthy sleep patterns. Develop a toolkit of bedtime rituals to promote peaceful sleep.

Afterword

We all come to earth to heal and to grow and evolve. Our wisdom and peace give us access to our greatest potential. We can be the beings of magnitude that we truly are.

Thank you, dear reader, for accompanying me on this healing journey towards wisdom and peace. I hope this book has helped you to remember that you are a spiritual being having an earthly experience. I hope that you access the wisdom you require to find the meaning and purpose for realising your dreams. Life can temporarily obscure our wisdom from us, as it can get buried under layers of our stuff. I hope the pearls of wisdom have helped you to find your own path to peace. I trust that some of which I have learned during this wonderful adventure called life has ignited your own inner wisdom and a desire for more. The keys to the kingdom really are found within and our own heaven on earth can exist. My wish for you is that, as you acquire the wisdom that best serves you on your journey, you carve out a beautiful life where peace reigns and your light shines. There is great peace in knowing one's wisdom is available at all times, in all situations. Your wisdom will lead you to your peace. May your peace allow your power, wisdom and potential to arise exponentially.

Love always, Jane x

Acknowledgements

This book is a culmination of my life experiences and the wisdom these 'blessings' have generated within. Thank you to all the 'characters' who have featured on my life stage, teaching me valuable lessons and helping me to discover my own light, wisdom and purpose.

Over many decades I've been drawn to the message of several writers and speakers. I would like to acknowledge them now for helping me shape my own vision of a life filled with wisdom and peace.

At first there was Oprah Winfrey, who encouraged my love of spirituality and personal growth. Next, along my journey came my 'Fab Four': Gabrielle Bernstein, who told me that the universe had my back and that I was a super attractor; Cassie Mendoza-Jones, who told me I was always enough and if I was aligned, I was unstoppable; Rebecca Campbell, who taught me to follow what lit me up and that I was a truly cosmic being; and Colette Baron-Reid, who inspired my love and affinity with oracle cards (particularly hers!).

Others of influence were: Marianne Williamson, who reminded me that I'm powerful beyond measure; Dr Wayne Dyer, always in the background with sage wisdom; Louise Hay, giving me advice on how to heal myself and my life; Dr Christiane Northrup, giving me back power over my health; Eckhart Tolle, delivering the importance and power of staying in the now; and Denise Linn, who encouraged my ability to connect to signs and the mystical and sacred.

I'd like to thank my beautiful daughter Julia, who is the earth angel that walks by my side, and my son Nic, who taught me about reaching for the stars, unconditional love and the power of surrender and faith.

Pete, my amazing husband, you taught me that my dreams counted and that they could come true. With you by my side everything has always been possible. You are the fairy tale and they do exist: my prince and my knight.

Dad, thank you for showing me the power of joy, laughter, fun, play, love, forgiveness and optimism. You let this daughter dream and forge her own path.

Mum, thank you for the safety you provided me as a child to grow and bloom and flourish. Your strength and patience against any odds, your resilience, consistency and unwavering support will stay with me always.

Lee, thank you for teaching me what only siblings can, and for embracing the love, support and loyalty that can exist within family.

Deb and Anne, I cherish our thirty-plus years of friendship. Thank you for embracing and supporting all the forks in the road I've taken.

Jane, thank you for knowing how to celebrate life anytime and anywhere and for sharing your beauty and light with me.

Thank you, my amazing Reiki One clients who were willing to do the brave inner work required to activate their personal wisdom, and to seek peace and all that that they desire in life. Many 'pearls' were inspired by the work and teachings we embraced.

Leah, thank you for being the first of my beautiful new tribe to arrive. I love your light, beauty and the way you respond to life.

Julia, thank you for your creativity and vision in organising my amazing book launch.

Sylvia, thank you for being an early pioneer with me into the world of energy healing and transformation. I loved our chapter—our seeking, our adventures and the wisdom-unlocking discussions we shared over a glass of wine.

Cassie Mendoza-Jones, thank you for your generosity of spirit, your insight and the energy of inspiration, hope and comfort you have provided for me on my writing journey. The universe sent me a writing angel.

Gary, you asked me once, many years ago, if I was willing for my writing ability of magnitude to show up. I stared at you blankly, as at the time I did not know that I was a writer and author. Obviously, you did! The answer is now yes, and thank you for asking. Much gratitude to you.

My 2019 Grade 5/6 literacy group members including Tamsyn, Bronte, Isabella, Meg, Sadie-May, Sophie, Annabelle, Lainee and Lil—thank you for your enthusiasm for the work that we created together. You regularly reignited my love of writing. I always loved that I finished my teaching career working with you. I can't wait to see what you create in the world.

Natasha, my publisher, thank you for recognising the potential for this book to make a difference in the world. I have been beautifully stunned by the flawless and seamless publishing journey I embarked on with you.

And lastly, love in white fur: Zoe and Mia, thank you for your unconditional love 24/7, and for the excitement you show every time you see me. You have been angelic constant companions. Yes, I can see your 'wings'.

About the Author

Jane Holman is a former primary school teacher who finished her teaching career to expand her love of writing and energy healing. Through her business, Reiki One, Jane conducts energy healing, intuitive counselling and life coaching whilst providing considerate direction and genuine motivation for aspiring writers. She loves facilitating people with their inner journeys towards wisdom, peace, power and potential. Seeing people transform and spread their wings lights her up.

Jane enjoys travel; being in nature, particularly on gorgeous beaches; swimming; self-care; Body Balance classes; making her home a sanctuary; fashion; and all things beautiful.

Jane lives on the north west coast of Tasmania. *Pearls of Wisdom: For Your Path to Peace* is her first book.

Website: janeholman.com.au
Facebook: Reiki One Jane Holman

www.ingramcontent.com/pod-product-compliance
Lightning Source LLC
Chambersburg PA
CBHW020313010526
44107CB00054B/1830